The Informability Manual

This manual is also available in braille and on audio cassette from the Customer Response Team, Royal National Institute for the Blind, PO Box 173, Peterborough PE2 6WS; tel: 01733 370777; fax: 01733 371555

The Informability Manual

Making information more accessible in the
light of the Disability Discrimination Act

London: HMSO

Researched and written by Wendy Gregory,
Informability Unit, Central Office of Information.

Illustrations by Barbara Baran.

Designed by Chris Davies,
Publications Division, Central Office of Information.

ISBN 0 11 702038 9

HMSO

HMSO publications are available from:

HMSO Publications Centre
(Mail, fax and telephone orders only)
PO Box 276, London SW8 5DT
Telephone orders 0171-873 9090
General enquiries 0171-873 0011
(queuing system in operation for
both numbers)
Fax orders 0171-873 8200

HMSO Bookshops
49 High Holborn, London WC1V 6HB
(counter service only)
0171-873 0011 Fax 0171-831 1326

68–69 Bull Street,
Birmingham B4 6AD
0121-236 9696 Fax 0121-236 9699

33 Wine Street, Bristol BS1 2BQ
0117 926 4306 Fax 0117 929 4515

9–21 Princess Street,
Manchester M60 8AS
0161-834 7201 Fax 0161-833 0634

16 Arthur Street, Belfast BT1 4GD
01232 238451 Fax 01232 235401

71 Lothian Road, Edinburgh EH3 9AZ
0131-479 3141 Fax 0131-479 3142

The HMSO Oriel Bookshop
The Friary, Cardiff CF1 4AA
01222 395548 Fax 01222 384347

HMSO's Accredited Agents
(see Yellow Pages)
and through good booksellers

Contents

USING THE INFORMABILITY MANUAL

Contents
The detailed contents list will help you find information quickly.

Cross references
Where a subject is covered in any detail in more than one part of the manual it is indicated by the further information logo and page numbers in the margin.

The arguments
Chapter 1 explains why anyone responsible for providing information should consider how best to make that information accessible to people who might otherwise not receive it.

The problems
Chapters 2–7 explain why certain conditions, disabilities or other problems can affect a person's ability to access information, and tell you which media will help overcome the difficulties.

The language
Chapter 8 is about using plain language – the most vitally important aspect of information provision, regardless of medium.

The solutions
Chapters 9–14 describe in more detail the media mentioned in the preceding chapters, and explain how the media can help to get messages across to a wider audience. These chapters also include summaries of how accessible each medium is to each of the groups described in chapters 2–7.

The appendices
Appendix 1 offers further statistics to reinforce and illustrate the points made throughout the book.

Appendix 2 gives some useful addresses and phone numbers.

Appendix 3 is a glossary of words and phrases relating to disability with some guidance on use. It also contains abbreviations used in the text.

Foreword

Informability is an initiative which, as a member of the general disability movement, I warmly welcome. Indeed, as someone who has been totally blind since I was eight years old, it is not surprising that I, and the Royal National Institute for the Blind, took it to our hearts when it was introduced in 1993.

Communication is fundamental for all human activity. To be able to express oneself in clear and intelligible language, to be assured that your message will be received, and to elicit a response, is an essential part of everyday life.

However, people have varying sensory perceptions of the world around them, varying abilities and disabilities and varying intellectual skills.

For too long, people with sight or hearing impairment and people who have difficulty reading have been overlooked by information providers. Not maliciously, simply from ignorance of the fact that these people want and need the same type and amount of information as everyone else.

Effective communication relies on an understanding of your audience and delivery of a clear message in a format that will be accessible and understood.

Fortunately times are changing. There is a growing willingness to consider the requirements of a wider spectrum of people. This is,

I believe, partly due to increased awareness and a genuine desire to help alleviate the problems experienced by some members of society. It is also partly due to increased commercial awareness. After all, elderly and disabled people constitute a growing proportion of the population and therefore a growing market to serve, and from which to profit.

Whatever the reasons, more information in accessible formats can only be a good thing.

The Informability Manual describes the audiences which need special consideration of their information needs and provides a good practice guide to the media best suited to meeting these needs. It is an invaluable tool for anyone wanting to improve their communication skills, and I'm delighted to have the opportunity to be able to recommend it to you.

John Wall CBE

Chairman, RNIB

Secretary General, European Blind Union

Chair, UK Helios Forum

Deputy Master of High Court, Chancery Divison

THE INFORMABILITY PRINCIPLE

It is obvious that everyone should be able to receive the information they want or need, in a manner and format they can understand; and that everyone should have access to the same quantity and quality of information at the same time as everyone else. This is the drum I've been beating ever since the Central Office of Information (COI) established the Informability Unit early in 1993.

The term 'informability' came into being one evening over supper at my kitchen table. It describes the principle of making information accessible to as many people as possible whatever their abilities or disabilities.

Whether in the private or the public sector, anyone with something to say, something to give, or something to sell will benefit from spreading their message more widely and more effectively.

This manual offers some basic guidelines to help them achieve this goal.

Of course, there is still a great deal more to be said and learnt about meeting the information needs of different types of people. As technology opens up so many exciting new channels of communication we all need to explore and develop ever more effective ways of delivering information.

To this end, we should all share our knowledge and experiences. Indeed, during the compilation of this manual, many people and organisations have kindly shared their knowledge and experiences with me.

Acknowledgements

I am especially grateful to John Wall CBE, Chairman of RNIB, for his support and for kindly agreeing to write the foreword.

I am also indebted to my colleagues in COI for all their help and encouragement. Very special thanks go to Don Low, whose vision led to Informability being born in the first place; and to designers Chris Davies and Steve Rigby who put so much thought and skill into the design and layout of the manual while remaining good natured and patient against all the odds.

Thanks to colleagues in various government departments who have shared their experiences of using accessible media and spoken frankly on departmental attitudes to accessible information provision.

Representatives of the major charities – especially the Royal National Institute for the Blind – have given freely of their time and advice on the basis that the manual is in line with their own aims. I hope their faith will be rewarded.

It isn't possible to name everyone who contributed or gave encouragement but much of the information contained in the manual came from people in the following organisations, some of whom also advised on parts of the text. I am very grateful to them all.

Age Concern

Basic Skills Agency

British Deaf Association

Citizen's Charter Unit

Deaf Broadcasting Council

Department of Health

Department of Social Security

Disability Information Service Surrey (DISS)

Disability Resource Team

Gateshead Libraries and Arts

Help the Aged

In Touch radio programme, BBC

London Deaf Access Project

Makaton Vocabulary Development Project

Mencap

Pia

Policy Studies Institute

RADAR

Royal National Institute for Deaf People

Royal National Institute for the Blind

See Hear! television programme, BBC

Sense

Southwark Inform

My thanks to everyone for all their help.

Wendy Gregory

Central Office of Information.

Chapter 1

ACCESSIBLE MEDIA: WHY BOTHER?

There are many reasons why people fail to receive or actively to seek information. For most of us there is an element of choice – we may choose not to watch the television, not to read the leaflet that comes through the door, or not to buy a newspaper. Everyone fails to get information they need at some time or another, but we can generally remedy the situation because we recognise the gaps in our knowledge and take steps to fill them.

For a significant minority this is not the case. Someone with below average reading ability, a limited understanding of English, or poor eyesight, may not find information in print very useful. Deaf or hard of hearing people may have difficulty with television or radio or using the telephone.

Because such people fail to receive a lot of general information they may be unaware of the very existence of certain topical issues, available products and services or legislation which affect their lives.

It is essential to remember that disabled people need much the same amount and type of information as everyone else.

The figures

A very large number of people are affected. In Britain there are:

- **over 7 million** adults with literacy problems;

- **1.7 million** people with visual impairment;

- **over 8 million** people with some form of hearing disability, including **62,000** who use British Sign Language as their preferred means of communication;

- **1 million** with learning difficulties (mental handicap).

Appendix 1 gives some more detailed figures.

People with disabilities are also consumers, employers, employees, parents, drivers, holiday-makers. The common attitude that they only need information when the message relates to disability, health or social service matters is clearly wrong, and patronising.

Enablement and empowerment – the goals of the champions of accessible media – come from having access to full, accurate and timely information, and result in increased independence and therefore less reliance on hard-stretched resources.

It is evident, however, that although many public and commercial organisations do accept the need to provide accessible information, by far the majority still do nothing, or very little, about it. And much information still fails to reach those who most need it.

A number of initiatives seek to change this situation. The most important of which is probably the Disability Discrimination Act 1995. In the light of this legislation, organisations will need to look much more carefully at making firm commitments to providing accessible information in the future.

Excuses, excuses . . .

A common excuse for not supplying information in alternative formats is that people who experience problems accessing that information can (or worse – should) rely on family, colleagues, friends or neighbours to interpret for them. This does often happen, but it is one of the major causes for complaints from people with disabilities. How would you like to ask a neighbour to read you a leaflet on contraception or AIDS, a letter from your bank manager, or a court summons?

Information providers need to address this situation and make improvements.

Commercial implications

Ensuring your information reaches a wider audience isn't just a politically correct gesture. The size of your potential audience means that it makes commercial sense too.

Certainly you should address blind or deaf people in a format they can understand so that they can comply with the law or claim benefit perhaps; but they are also consumers like everyone else. If you take the trouble to tell these audiences about your products or services they will choose them rather than those of your competitors.

General audiences

An added bonus is that by following many of the guidelines on producing accessible information for particular groups, you also benefit a wider audience.

For instance:

- Using plain language makes information easier for everyone to understand, and is usually shorter and therefore cheaper to produce than bureaucratic language.

- Using a clear typeface makes a printed document easier to read for everyone.

10, 53

Ethnic languages

There are also 2.6 million members of ethnic minority groups, who may need information in their own language. In addition to this, the Welsh Language Act (1993) has already established the rights of Welsh speakers to receive information in Welsh.

This manual does not cover ethnic issues, but what is true for the majority of the population also applies to those who do not speak or read English. Literacy problems, poor eyesight or hearing recognise no cultural boundaries.

informability

For 50 years, the role of the Central Office of Information (COI) has been to help ensure the widespread availability of full and accurate public sector information. In recent years, in line with the aims of the Citizen's Charter, COI realised that its responsibility should also be actively to promote the use of accessible media and to make the best use of them.

Early in 1993, COI set up a research project to examine the most effective methods of information provision. From this project the Informability Unit was born.

The Unit was established to offer advice on ways of improving government communication using a range of media techniques. It works in consultation with colleagues in COI and in government departments and agencies, and with representatives of charitable and other organisations.

Research

It is essential to understand the problems before you can begin to address them, so our initial research had five main aims:

- To identify and quantify which conditions and disabilities may affect an individual's ability to access information.

- To examine the relative merits of the media which can facilitate access to such information.

- To assess how far government departments and other organisations already meet the needs of the people identified.

- To canvass opinion within government and specialist organisations, including charities, on how information provision might be improved.

- To examine existing expertise in procuring and distributing information in accessible media.

A subsidiary aim was to start collecting hard facts, statistics and contact names and addresses, which would:

- Demonstrate the importance of catering for the special groups in information campaigns.

- Form a pool of information to help COI provide the most effective advice and procurement services to its clients.

In an ideal world all information would be available in whichever format each individual prefers. In practice, however, resources are always limited. Therefore the Informability Unit also looks for economical ways of communicating more effectively through existing channels, and identifying where savings can be made to free up resources to invest in more accessible media.

The Informability Guide

Having examined the facts, the Informability Unit was able to begin offering advice and practical help to colleagues in COI and to COI's public sector clients. It was for this reason that in 1993 we published *The Informability Guide* to help and encourage our colleagues in the public sector to expand their audiences and increase the effectiveness of their messages. We hoped that the *Guide* would help explain to those not yet convinced of the arguments that it is essential to consider their information strategies in a broader field.

Since we published the *Guide*, the Disability Discrimination Act 1995 has made it all the more essential for service and information providers everywhere to examine how they can best meet the information needs of disabled people. We therefore decided to make our research findings available to a wider audience by compiling *The Informability Manual*.

The information contained in the *Guide* has been revised, expanded and brought up to date in *The Informability Manual*. New material in the manual includes the chapters on telephones, plain language and signage; practical guidelines on writing in plain language, designing for large print, and preparing material for audio tape; and lists of helpful statistics and addresses.

THE DISABILITY DISCRIMINATION ACT

The Disability Discrimination Act 1995 (DDA) prohibits discrimination against disabled people in the provision of goods or services. The Act makes it clear that access to and use of information and communication services are covered by the right of access to goods and services. This includes services provided by the public as well as by the private sector and individuals.

Implementation of the Act is being phased in over several years, and it is not clear (at the time of writing) exactly what its impact on service providers or disabled people will be. However, basically, the DDA will impose four broad duties on service providers:

- It will be unlawful to refuse a service to a disabled person for reasons relating to their disability.

- There will be an obligation to adjust policies, practices and procedures where these make it unreasonably difficult or impossible for a disabled person to use the service.

- There will be a duty to provide auxiliary aids and services such as the provision of information in accessible media such as braille and audio tape for blind people, or the installation of induction loops to assist people with hearing aids.

- There will be a duty to remove physical barriers wherever reasonable or to provide a service by alternative means.

In cases of alleged discrimination, people with disabilities will be able to take their complaints to court.

The implementation of the DDA has major implications for many information and service providers, who will be required to make their services accessible to a much wider audience.

UN STANDARD RULES

The *United Nations Standard Rules for the Equalisation of Opportunities for Disabled People* also relate to the accessiblity of information and communication. The standard rules were adopted by the UN General Assembly in December 1993. Although they are not legally binding, the rules urge member states to participate in actively improving the living conditions of disabled people globally and to increase the opportunities for people with disabilities to enjoy active participation in society.

Rule 5(b) states:

- Persons with disabilities and, where appropriate, their families and advocates should have access to full information on diagnosis, rights and available services and programmes, at all stages. Such information should be presented in forms accessible to people with disabilities.

- States should develop strategies to make information services and documentation accessible for different groups of people with disabilities. Braille, tape services, large print and other appropriate technologies should be used to provide access to written information and documentation for persons with visual impairments. Similarly, appropriate technologies should be used to provide access to spoken information for persons with auditory impairments or comprehension difficulties.

- Sign language interpretation services should also be provided to facilitate the communication between deaf persons and others.

- Consideration should also be given to the needs of people with other communication disabilities.

- States should encourage the media, especially television, radio and newspapers, to make their services accessible.

- States should ensure that new computerised information and service systems offered to the general public are either made initially accessible or are adapted to be made accessible to persons with disabilities.

COMMITMENT TO THE CAUSE

In Britain, especially in view of the DDA, there is a great deal of discussion and research throughout the public and private sectors into improving information and communication in general for people with disabilities.

The Minister for Disabled People, hundreds of charities, lobby groups, commercial organisations and many politicians strive towards a better-informed future.

The European Union is also committed to the cause. It has a number of projects and grants aimed at enabling disabled and elderly people to live full, independent lives. The TIDE (Telematics applications for the Integration of Disabled and Elderly people) programme in particular funds dozens of projects to promote research and technological development to help meet the needs of older and disabled people and to help them live autonomously and participate more fully in the social and economic life of the community.

In the European Parliament, the Disability Inter-group includes MEPs of all political persuasions working together.

It is vital that we all share our experiences if we are to use limited resources more effectively.

The case for providing accessible information is indisputable. The following chapters explain the problems and offer advice on how to overcome them:

Chapter 2

PEOPLE WITH LITERACY PROBLEMS

Around 7.3 million adults – or 16 per cent of the adult population – in the UK are estimated to have difficulties with reading, writing or basic arithmetic. Age, gender, employment and socio-economic background can all affect a person's level of literacy. The Basic Skills Agency's survey *Older and Younger: the basic skills of different age groups* (1995) found, for instance, that on average people in their 20s have poorer literacy skills than those in their 40s, and that those over 70 scored lowest.

There is a wide range of literacy problems – from people who can read reasonably well but have poor spelling or writing, through to those who can barely read or write at all. The majority can read basic texts but have difficulty with forms, official correspondence and legal material. Relatively few adults are completely illiterate and therefore cannot read at all.

A survey carried out by The Basic Skills Agency in 1995 found that 25 per cent of adults tested on their ability to fill in a form could only give very basic information – such as their name and address – and made significant mistakes in grammar and spelling.

Someone with poor reading skills faces all kinds of problems. They may not be able to follow instructions on medicine bottles, complete a ballot paper or understand road signs. Understanding long or complicated documents, such as insurance policies or mortgage agreements, can be virtually impossible.

A major problem when providing information in a form that will be useful to this group is that its members will often not admit their difficulties. This hidden audience could include one in six of the adult population – a sizeable minority which should not be overlooked or ignored.

3, 53

People from ethnic minorities who understand spoken English but cannot read or write it could be considered as part of this group. However, they may well be literate in their own language and would therefore benefit more from information supplied in that language.

USEFUL MEDIA

Obviously the printed word is not the most user-friendly medium for people with literacy problems but it will often be the only option available. So it is important to write simply and clearly.

Also, many of the techniques which help people with hearing or visual problems, people with learning difficulties and some older people to understand information will also benefit those with reading difficulties.

However, the fact that many people do not admit to having a problem with literacy requires sensitive handling by copywriters and designers.

It is rarely a good idea to suggest that your information has been specially prepared for people who have literacy problems.

Printed material

64

The Adult Literacy and Basic Skills Unit (now The Basic Skills Agency) guidelines give advice on producing printed material for people with literacy problems. They state that 'the type most suitable for adults should be clear and legible, rather than large'. When you address an adult audience, it is obviously important that your text should not look as if it has been designed for children.

Printed material should be:

■ in plain language;

■ as concise as possible; and

■ in clear type (but not too large).

Following these basic rules will also aid comprehension for a number of other groups.

54 The general guidelines on plain language will help you provide documents that are more accessible to people with literacy problems. But it is important to remember that type which is too large, or language which is too simplistic, can suggest that the text is intended for children or for people with learning difficulties, and so alienate the adult reader.

Design and layout

For many adults, problems with reading result from the appearance and layout of the book or leaflet. Design features, such as printing text on top of images, or positioning columns or lines of text too closely together, can create barriers to comprehension.

Illustrations, photographs, cartoons and diagrams can help keep text to a minimum, make the message clearer, and the material more attractive and user-friendly. This is true for most audiences, not just for those with literacy problems.

Broadcast media

Television and radio

80, 92 Both TV and radio are major information sources for this group because the information is verbal and visual rather than text-based.

Video and audio tape

82, 87 Video and audio tapes can be useful for the same reasons as TV and radio, but be careful when labelling tapes to avoid suggesting that they are aimed at 'disabled' or 'mentally handicapped' people.

Multi-media

94

A growing number of households now have computers and compact disc (CD) players and access to the Internet, as do many organisations such as libraries, offices and schools. So opportunities for delivering information in forms which rely less on the written word are increasing all the time.

CD-I (CD interactive) and CD-ROM (CD read-only memory) can supply an interactive mix of sound, pictures and text. And many computer programmes rely to a greater or lesser degree on icon recognition rather than the ability to read.

However, modern technology is not available to many people because of its high cost and complexity. Although they may sometimes be useful, electronic media should not be seen as alternatives to more traditional information sources but as potentially useful additions to them.

Telephones

102

For someone who has difficulty reading, the spoken word will always be more useful. You will help people with literacy difficulties if you can offer telephone helplines, or direct access by telephone to people who are able to supply information.

TARGETING INFORMATION

Targeting information is difficult because of the unwillingness of people with literacy difficulties to admit their special needs.

However, if you keep information in print simple, and therefore more accessible to everyone, it is also more likely to be understood by people in this group.

You should offer other media, such as audio tape, as alternative sources of information, rather than suggesting that they are aimed specifically at people who are illiterate or who have a sight impairment for instance.

Chapter 3

PEOPLE WHO ARE DEAF OR HARD OF HEARING

The Royal National Institute for Deaf People (RNID) estimates that around 8.4 million adults in Britain are deaf or hard of hearing. This figure represents the whole spectrum of hearing impairment from profound or prelingual deafness to people who are slightly hard of hearing or have become deaf gradually with age. Of these 8.4 million people, some 250,000 have profound hearing loss, and 420,000 are unable to use a voice telephone even if it is adapted to amplify sound.

'Profound deafness' means that a person has no useful hearing. 'Prelingual deafness' means they were born deaf or lost their hearing before they learnt to speak.

It is generally accepted among organisations and people involved with sensory impairment that deafness affects a person's life even more significantly than blindness. This is due to the isolating effect of deafness. A person who is blind can still communicate with others through the spoken word, whereas a person who is deaf or hard of hearing is more cut off.

The major sources of aural communication – speech, telephones, television and radio – present problems for people who have a hearing impairment. This can lead to dramatic gaps in the type and amount of information they receive in the course of day-to-day living. Information considered common knowledge by the majority of the population may be unknown to Deaf people. (See the Glossary for the distinction between 'Deaf' and 'deaf'.) Deaf parents of hearing children may be unaware, for instance, of the existence of the National Curriculum, let alone know the details of how it works.

The Deaf Community

Many people who are Deaf do not regard themselves as disabled by their deafness but by society's inability to recognise and deal with the differences between the needs of 'culturally' Deaf and

hearing people. Culturally Deaf people consider themselves part of a linguistic, cultural minority group – the Deaf community. They use British Sign Language (BSL), which is commonly their first language, and therefore the one they understand best.

16 ℹ

They may also use other communication systems such as Sign Supported English (SSE) or fingerspelling.

17 ℹ

The Deaf community is just that – a distinct community. It has its own language, social and information network, customs, rules of etiquette, and sense of community. It is important to remember this when considering how best to present and disseminate information to people who are culturally Deaf.

A common misconception is that there is no need to make special provision for people with hearing problems as they should be able to gain information from the printed word. This is often untrue. The average reading age of profoundly or severely Deaf school-leavers is less than nine years old. This is not generally due to lack of academic potential but to the fact that the 62,000 prelingually Deaf people in the UK learn and use BSL as their first language. Their understanding of English is often limited.

This has important implications. Written information is less accessible, and there is a 'hidden' problem in that many Deaf people are embarrassed by their poor spelling and grammar, and are therefore loath to write, or even to use textphones, to communicate with hearing people.

For these reasons, Deaf people may become isolated from the rest of the community and therefore doubly unlikely to receive information which they need.

People who are hard of hearing

Most deafened and hard of hearing people, however, do not consider themselves part of this community since English is their first language.

For people who are deaf or hard of hearing but literate in English there are no greater problems accessing printed information than for anyone else. Their problems arise with sound-based information sources such as TV and radio.

Sixty per cent of people with hearing impairment are over 70 and are therefore likely to have other disabilities as well as deafness. For instance, their eyesight may also have deteriorated.

80, 100

British Sign Language (BSL)

BSL is a language of gestures and facial expression. It can only be used face to face, on video or using electronic media such as CD-I. It has its own grammar and cannot be written down. It is not possible to translate English precisely, word for word, into BSL.

This has important implications for the information provider. You will need to employ qualified translators to convert your texts accurately into BSL. You will also need to be prepared to discuss how to present words and concepts which have no exact equivalent in BSL.

In order to make the process as simple as possible, it is important to keep messages clear and succinct.

Although BSL cannot be written down the *Dictionary of British Sign Language/English* (Faber and Faber) is a useful reference work for students of BSL. It uses photographs, symbols and written descriptions to relate BSL signs to the most commonly used English words.

Sign Supported English (SSE)

Some signing systems have developed which incorporate elements of BSL, fingerspelling and English together. These systems typically follow the grammatical structure and word order of spoken English, but are not as flexible or expressive as BSL. Examples include Sign Supported English, Signed English and British Signed English.

Fingerspelling

The English fingerspelling system uses a two-handed alphabet. Other nationalities have different systems. The Irish, for instance, use a one-handed alphabet. Fingerspelling is used by all signers to a greater or lesser degree to indicate words, such as proper names, which do not have a dedicated sign.

Face-to-face communication

Sometimes you may need to communicate with deaf or hard of hearing people individually or in small groups. Occasions such as:

- meeting with or providing a service to members of the public;

- interviewing a job applicant; or

- accommodating deaf participants at a meeting or conference.

On these occasions it is important to recognise the problems deaf or hard of hearing people may encounter. You will need to find out what facilities the individual(s) concerned need, and provide them.

You will need to:

- contact the deaf or hard of hearing people to establish what special arrangements they may want;

- arrange seating so that they can see speakers' faces and sign language interpreters clearly;

- encourage other participants to speak one at a time, to face the audience and speak clearly (without exaggerated lip movements);

- provide suitable lighting so speakers and interpreters are well lit without dazzling those who need to see them clearly.

You may also need to:

- choose a quiet room without background noise;

- provide an induction loop system for people with hearing aids;

- offer to provide facilities for the deaf person to bring their own interpreter. Or yourself provide one or more BSL or SSE interpreters, lip speakers or palantypists (someone who types what is said onto a special machine which then projects the text on to a screen) as required;

- provide written information such as the agenda or speakers' notes in advance;

- encourage staff or others to undergo disability or deaf awareness training to help them provide a better service.

Lip reading

Many people who are deaf or hard of hearing can receive spoken information if the speaker enunciates well and their lips are clearly visible. However, a good lip reader needs skill, patience and often training to master the technique properly. It is also very tiring to have to lip read for long stretches of time.

When producing videos for people with a hearing impairment it is important that speakers' faces and lips are clearly visible.

Trained lip speakers can provide a valuable interpreting service.

Induction loops and infra-red systems

A major obstacle to understanding speech is background noise. Hearing aids amplify all sound which means speech can often be distorted or drowned out.

An induction loop is a coil of wire round a room or area which transmits audio frequencies by means of a magnetic field. An induction loop amplifies sound and also reduces background noise. Users of hearing aids within the loop must set their aids to the 'T' setting to receive the transmission.

Induction loops can be permanently installed, or there are portable versions available which can be moved from room to room.

Installing induction loops or infra-red systems in public places such as exhibitions, theatres or interview rooms assists some hearing-aid users. Smaller loops may be used in places like railway booking offices and banks.

Infra-red systems perform much the same function using beams of infra-red light.

Always remember to inform people that a loop has been provided so that they know they can use it if they wish.

USEFUL MEDIA

You can meet the information needs of people who are deaf or hard of hearing in several ways.

People who are prelingually Deaf generally prefer to receive information in BSL, whereas someone who becomes deafened later in life is likely to prefer printed information or a subtitled video. Remember also that many of these people may not have perfect eyesight.

19

64

Standard print

Most people who are hard of hearing can read, so printed information is acceptable. However, many older people, who may also have poor sight, fall into this category, so you should think carefully about design and about where and how to distribute the publication.

There are several magazines and newsletters specifically for deaf and hard of hearing people, both in printed form and on teletext.

80–83, 99

Television, video and compact disc

For profoundly and prelingually Deaf people who use BSL as their first language, the only way to receive readily accessible information is through BSL. The very nature of BSL as a distinct visual-gestural language precludes the use of static media such as print. It can only be used on broadcast television, or recorded on video or CD-I or CD-ROM.

These are relatively expensive options, so you should take them into account at the earliest possible stage when calculating your publicity budgets.

When producing BSL videos it is desirable to use experienced Deaf people and others used to working with them. Effective communication does not just rely on technical ability but on an understanding of Deaf culture and language.

It can be expensive to produce material in BSL because of the number of people and amount of time needed to ensure accuracy. English text must be translated into BSL, and then checked and the delivery of the translation monitored. (The principles and problems are much the same as with translation from one spoken language to another.) This means that a Deaf video production crew involves several more members than its hearing equivalent.

You will also need to include extra time in the schedule to allow for translating and checking the script, resolving difficult words or concepts and possibly clearing the final translation of the script with your clients or policy makers.

The British Deaf Association (BDA) recommends that signers should be Deaf, fluent, native users of BSL.

Television and video subtitling

83

Although around 4.2 million people have difficulty understanding speech on television, most people who are deaf or hard of hearing have a TV set. Indeed, according to the Broadcasters Audience Research Bureau, 10 million viewers currently watch subtitles.

Subtitling can be either 'open' which means it appears on the screen automatically, or 'closed' where a special decoder is needed to display the subtitles. Closed subtitling has the advantage of allowing viewers to choose whether they want to use the subtitles or not.

Although it is possible to add both BSL and subtitles to existing video this can lead to poor quality, and is complicated and expensive. It is better to plan to include BSL and subtitles from the start of a project.

Adding BSL to existing video material

It is possible to add BSL translation to existing recordings as an inset in the corner of the picture. However, take care. The framing of a pre-existing recording may not comfortably adapt to having part of the screen obscured by the inset. Nor is this technique an ideal solution because:

■ The interpreter will be small in relation to the rest of the picture.

■ The original recording may deliver information too quickly to allow an accurate translation to be superimposed.

■ The combined effect of action on the screen and the moving signer may make it difficult for Deaf people to take in all of the information at once.

Teletext

85

Teletext services are useful sources of information because they can be called up when needed and examined at leisure.

Textphones

102

Textphones enable people who are deaf or hard of hearing to communicate using text via the telephone. The user types their message on a keyboard linked to the telephone and the message then appears on a small screen at the other end of the line.

If information providers offer a textphone facility it gives people with speech or hearing difficulties the same telephone access to information, goods or services as the rest of the population.

Typetalk

102

If you cannot offer a textphone service, then recommending using the Typetalk service will make telephone access easier for many deaf and hard of hearing people.

Typetalk is a service which enables people with textphones to communicate with ordinary telephone users, and vice versa, through an operator who acts as an intermediary.

104

Videophones

Videophones are not, as yet, generally available. However, once the technology has advanced and image quality improved, people who use sign language will benefit dramatically from a telephone system which allows them to see the person at the other end of the line.

Apart from being able to communicate with other sign language users, it would also become possible, in theory, for Deaf and hearing people to communicate through an operator-interpreter along the same lines as the existing Typetalk system.

TARGETING INFORMATION

Thanks to the existence of a distinct Deaf community, it is possible accurately to target specially produced material, such as videos, at Deaf clubs and other Deaf organisations. This can be done relatively cheaply through organisations such as the BDA.

You should publicise the existence of accessible material in deaf publications and programmes and in more generally targeted literature, with details of how to obtain it.

There are a few TV programmes in the UK specially for people who are deaf or hard of hearing, such as the BBC's *See Hear!* and *See Hear Breakfast News* and Tyne Tees' *Sign On*, networked nationally on Channel 4. The BBC and a growing number of regional ITV companies broadcast news digests for people who are deaf or hard of hearing. These programmes can be useful conduits for information, although they are not necessarily broadcast continuously throughout the year.

Targeting information precisely at people who are hard of hearing is less easy. However, most hard of hearing people will receive information through a variety of the same sources used by the population in general.

104

If you give a telephone number in the standard literature, you should also offer a textphone number, and/or the Typetalk number.

23

Chapter 4

PEOPLE WHO ARE BLIND OR PARTIALLY SIGHTED

Around 1.1 million people in Britain are estimated to have a visual impairment severe enough to be eligible for registration as blind or partially sighted, and 1.7 million are estimated to find it difficult or impossible to read ordinary newspaper print.

However, the number of people who experience problems due to poor eyesight is much greater than these figures suggest. There is no legal requirement to register and most people do not. Many people simply accept failing eyesight as a consequence of ageing.

There are many types and effects of blindness. Some people have tunnel vision, others see only at the periphery of their field of vision; some see everything as a blur, or with bits of their field of vision missing; while others can only distinguish dark from light. Four per cent of blind people have no light perception and therefore can see nothing at all.

> You cannot stereotype blind people. They do not all have a guide dog, carry a white stick or wear dark glasses.

Distribution of visual impairment is, however, heavily biased towards older people: almost 90 per cent are over 60, including three quarters of a million over 75. The majority experience a progressive, relatively protracted deterioration of sight over the years, and many older people have other disabilities, including hearing problems.

Forty-five per cent of people with visual impairment live alone and many are housebound.

USEFUL MEDIA

People with visual impairment cannot be viewed as an homogeneous mass. A document in large print is no use to a braille reader, nor is a printed document designed for use by someone with glaucoma (which affects peripheral vision) likely to be helpful to someone with macular disease (which affects central vision).

No one special medium will be accessible to everyone with visual impairment, so you should always try to produce information in a number of media whenever possible.

Some blind people, especially those with little or no sight, use braille or Moon, which are tactile alphabets. Some find audio tape convenient, others are satisfied with large print or will use a personal computer (PC) to convert information into an accessible format. Their preference may also vary according to the type and length of the material they want to access.

Standard print

64

The Royal National Institute for the Blind (RNIB) survey *Blind and partially sighted adults in Britain* (HMSO 1991) concluded that 48 per cent of blind or partially sighted adults are able to read standard print. However, it would be unwise to assume that 48 per cent can do so with ease, especially if the document is very long, poorly designed or badly printed.

To ensure that standard print is legible for as wide an audience as possible RNIB recommend a minimum type size of 12 pt. You can also greatly increase legibility if you take some of the guidelines for large print design into account when preparing your standard print documents. This manual is set in 12pt Century Book with 3pt leading.

Large/clear print

66

There is currently some debate as to whether the term 'large print' or 'clear print' is the more appropriate. In this manual I have chosen to use 'large print' when referring to type that is 14pt and above. It goes without saying that large print should also be 'clear' if it is to achieve its purpose.

Accurate figures on how many people who are blind or partially sighted and can read large print are hard to establish. The RNIB survey suggests that a significant proportion – 36 per cent of blind and 75 per cent of partially sighted people – are able to read large print (with varying degrees of ease).

However, the effectiveness of large print, although significant, should not be over-estimated. Although a relatively large number of people can decipher words in large print, many cannot comfortably read a whole leaflet or tackle a book.

Modified print

Some people with severe visual impairment can access information in print if it is adapted for their specific needs. Modifications vary from individual to individual, but could include:

- using a particular type size or style;

- enlarging or simplifying illustrations or diagrams;

- describing visual elements of the document in words.

It is rarely practical to mass produce documents in modified print as each person will have particular needs. If you need to provide such documents it is best to seek professional advice.

Braille

73

There are around 19,000 braille readers in Britain, 13,000 of whom are active readers. They tend to be people who were born blind, or became blind at an early age. For those who read braille it is usually their preferred method of receiving and storing information.

110

Many other blind and partially sighted people make use of braille labelling on, for instance, packaging, signposting and lift buttons.

Although this is a relatively small group, a different picture of the importance of braille emerges when the figures are examined: braille is accessible to over 20 per cent of people of working age who are registrable as blind.

Braille readers are often the most influential or most active members of the blind community. They are therefore useful channels of information for other blind people. To quote RNIB: 'such active representatives can be thought of as the top of the VI [visually impaired] grapevine'.

This group has a particularly acute need for information in an accessible medium to allow its members to take an active role in everyday life. They demand and, most importantly, use braille. Their specialised needs should not therefore be discounted due to low numbers.

Braille can make all kinds of documents accessible:

- books;

- magazines;

- leaflets;

- bank statements;

- bills from the public utilities;

- knitting patterns;

- sheet music;

and all kinds of other information usually produced in print can be transcribed into braille.

One of the reasons that braille is read by relatively few people is that so little is produced as a matter of course. Even when it is, it is rarely available at the same time as its print counterpart. However, as more braille documents are becoming available demand is increasing and it is likely that the number of braille readers will also increase.

Meanwhile, many braille readers will continue to wait weeks or even years for information to be transcribed for them.

Moon

79

Moon is a simple tactile alphabet used by an estimated 1,000 people – usually elderly people as it requires less sensitivity in the finger tips. It has similarities to the Roman alphabet and is therefore much easier to learn than braille for someone who has been familiar with the printed word.

It is, however, a very bulky medium and the number of readers is small and relatively static.

Television, video and audio description

80, 82, 84

Some 90 per cent of blind and partially sighted people 'watch' television, and 60 per cent say that it is one of their most important sources of information. For them, television or video can be greatly enhanced by adding an audio description channel. This is a separate broadcast channel which carries a sound track that gives additional information about the visual detail appearing on the screen.

84

The system was the subject of an EC-funded research project – Audetel – which ran trial broadcasts in the UK in 1994.

There is a growing trend for popular videos to be produced with audio description.

As the technology develops, audio description may well become a more important source of information for people with a visual impairment.

Radio

92

Sixty-two per cent of people who are blind or partially sighted rate radio as one of their most important sources of information. Local radio is particularly effective.

There are also a few programmes, such as BBC Radio 4's *In Touch*, which specifically address the visually impaired community.

87

Audio tape

Audio tape can be a useful medium provided, of course, that the recipient has a tape player. Age is a major influencing factor: 67 per cent of visually impaired under-60s have a tape player, but only 29 per cent of retired people. This gap is narrowing as generations grow up accustomed to the technology.

RNIB's survey found that there is a significant difference between actual and potential use of tape as an accessible medium. Although many blind and partially sighted people own tape players they are more likely to use them for leisure purposes than for accessing information. This is partly because in the past little information was actually available on tape. Also, many people do not find tape a very convenient medium. It is more difficult to navigate through information on tape than in braille or large print. However, the increasing availability today of more taped information will undoubtedly lead to more use.

32

Certain taped material for blind people can be sent post-free under the Royal Mail 'Articles for the Blind' scheme.

Electronic aids

A number of electronic aids assist access to information. People who can afford them increasingly own personal computers and many more have access to them in their workplace. This means that information supplied on disc or via the Internet is becoming increasingly useful to those people who have access to the technology to convert it to a convenient format.

Special software can enable visually impaired people to translate information from a variety of sources into accessible formats. For instance, it is possible to convert text in print or from the Internet into speech or braille.

Scanners (often called Optical Character Readers or OCRs) can display printed text in an enlarged form on the computer screen or store it as a computer readable file.

Closed Circuit Televisions (CCTVs) can be used to magnify print and graphics onto a screen or computer monitor.

Soft/renewable braille read-outs (movable pins on a special display linked to a computer) enable braille readers to read text from a computer disc.

Braille embossers can convert text on disc or from the Internet to pages of braille.

Speech synthesisers will read text aloud from scanned text or from a computer file.

Information on disc can be enlarged on screen by many PCs.

Tactile reading aids scan text and graphic images and convert them to a tactile image which can be 'read' with a finger tip.

On-line information: *The Guardian* was the first daily newspaper to be transmitted down telephone lines at night to PCs. This gives people who are blind the possibility of accessing daily news coverage at the same time as – or earlier than – sighted people. This development heralds a new era of electronic publishing which will undoubtedly become a significant information tool in future.

Graphical User Interfaces (GUIs): Many computer programmes use GUIs. These can be useful for partially sighted people using magnification software. But GUIs can present problems for some people with a visual impairment because their operation relies on icons and images rather than text. Some software can, however, also make GUIs accessible through speech synthesisers or braille, but the software can be difficult to use. This problem is the subject of much research, and will no doubt be overcome in time.

The Internet can be a useful information source for some blind and partially sighted people. However, neither speech nor braille can interpret images. If an image has an associated text label describing the image its existence and content then become accessible.

31

Telephone helplines

Telephone helplines such as the enquiry line operated by the Benefits Agency are especially useful for blind and partially sighted people. However, as 25 per cent of blind and partially sighted people do not have telephones (compared to 12 per cent of the population as a whole) helplines may not be universally accessible to blind people.

Again, you should publicise the availability of telephone response or helplines to make sure that your audience knows about them.

Articles for the Blind

The Royal Mail's 'Articles for the Blind' scheme allows various items, including braille and audio tape, to be sent by first class post to blind people for free provided they are

- marked as 'Articles for the Blind';

- exact transcriptions of the printed material; and

- packed to allow inspection by the Post Office.

However, the rules governing the service are complex, so it is best to check with the Royal Mail before using the service.

TARGETING INFORMATION

You should always try to ensure that you make the alternative formats available at the same time as the standard print version.

There is no point in producing accessible formats if no one knows they are available. As with any information, you should always publicise the availability of alternative formats such as braille, audio tape and/or large print. They should always be mentioned in the standard print literature, in any other formats, and in catalogues of publications. It is also useful if you can promote them in recognised sources of information for visually impaired people such as publications or radio programmes specially for people who are blind or partially sighted.

These days, many libraries offer large print, audio tape and braille sections. The *Share the Vision* project encourages libraries to provide special services for people with visual impairment and also promotes the services.

If you offer information in response to filling in a form, always ensure that the form is produced in an adequate type size and allows plenty of room to accommodate large handwriting.

Organisations and charities of and for people with visual impairment can help you to target people who are blind or partially sighted or the organisations representing them.

If the likely demand for braille, tape or large print is unknown, it may be possible to provide these formats on request using in-house technology or small local suppliers.

For the 45 per cent of people with visual impairment who live alone, many of whom are housebound, their isolation has significant implications for information- and service-providers. You cannot assume that someone else will pass information on to them as a matter of course. However, specific targeting of sighted carers of blind people (professional and voluntary) can prove effective for disseminating certain types of information.

Chapter 5

PEOPLE WHO ARE DEAF-BLIND

There may be as many as 250,000 deaf-blind people in Britain, including over 23,000 who are severely affected by the condition.

The term 'deaf-blind' (or dual-sensory impaired) doesn't usually mean totally deaf and totally blind, although such conditions do exist. It denotes a combination of visual and auditory impairments which cause unique problems in communication, receiving information and understanding it.

The causes of deaf-blindness include maternal rubella (German measles) and Usher syndrome, but the majority of people simply have varying degrees of impaired vision and hearing due to a variety of causes.

The precise number of people in Britain who are deaf-blind is unclear because deaf-blindness often occurs with disabilities such as mental handicap which can mask the sensory impairment.

The figure quoted by Sense, the charity for deaf-blind people, is over 23,000, but the RNIB's survey (1991) found 22 per cent of visually impaired people under 60 also suffer the additional disadvantage of having difficulties with hearing; this figure rises to a possible 45 per cent of those over 75. The total number of people with some degree of both hearing and visual impairment then, according to RNIB, is 250,000. The large discrepancy between these figures is due to the difference in the two organisations' definitions of the disabilities.

The RNIB survey concluded: 'People and organisations who work with very old visually impaired people may assume that half are hard of hearing. Communication with such individuals needs to be assessed in the light of this information.'

USEFUL MEDIA

Where one or other (or both) of the impairments is not a total loss of sensory faculty, and assuming no mental disability, the techniques described in the chapters on hearing and visual impairment, and on older people, will also be useful for delivering information to deaf-blind people.

The National Deaf-Blind League recommends the following media as being accessible to some deaf-blind people:

73

66

79

87

20

102

- braille;

- large print;

- Moon;

- clear speech on cassette; and

- signed communication on video.

Telephone communication through Typetalk operators can also be helpful to those deaf-blind people who are familiar with written and spoken English and provided they have enough useful sight to use a textphone, or they have access to an adapted textphone which allows communication in braille.

TARGETING INFORMATION

Provided you ensure your information is available in a variety of media useful to people with visual or hearing impairment, some deaf-blind people will benefit, depending on the extent of their disability .

People with severe deaf-blindness – generally those represented by Sense – can only receive information on a one-to-one basis. This requires a trained signer either to spell out messages in the deaf-blind manual alphabet on the person's hands; or to sign in BSL, or other appropriate sign language, while the person who is deaf-blind grips the signer's arms to follow the movements.

Many severely deaf-blind people, especially those with mental handicaps, live in sheltered or medical institutions. In these circumstances it is most effective for information providers to target carers, and medical and social workers.

Chapter 6

PEOPLE WITH LEARNING DIFFICULTIES

Over 1 million people in Britain have some degree of learning difficulty.

There is scope for confusion over this term:

- 'People with learning difficulties' is the generally accepted term for those adults still sometimes known as mentally handicapped. You should, however, avoid the term 'mental handicap' as it is not generally acceptable to people with learning difficulties.

- The charity Mencap uses 'learning disabilities'.

- The Department for Education uses 'learning difficulties' to describe any child with 'special educational needs', which by its definition includes children with mental handicaps, behavioural problems, sensory impairment, literacy problems and physical disabilities.

Many people with learning difficulties also have other disabilities; the more severe the learning difficulty, the greater the likelihood of additional physical or sensory disability.

Since this manual deals with information provision to adults unlikely to be severely mentally handicapped, we use the term 'learning difficulties' as being the most accurate and the most acceptable to the people concerned.

What are learning difficulties?

'Mental handicap' is a condition caused by damage to a person's brain before or at birth, or during childhood, by a range of factors including genetic ones. People with this condition cannot be cured, but they can achieve varying degrees of competence and independence with appropriate support and training. The condition should not be confused with mental illness, which affects people across the whole range of intelligence and which may be successfully treated, and in many cases cured.

43

'People with learning difficulties' is a term covering a broad range of people, from those capable of living independently and holding down a job given a little support, to people who can do little for themselves and need a lot of care and support.

The right to information

In the past, many people with learning difficulties lived in institutions – hospitals or special homes. Today, many live in the community where they want and need a variety of information and opportunities in forms they can readily access. The information they need won't necessarily relate directly to their particular problems – many need much the same sort of information as the rest of the population. But it is important to ensure that the information is timely, relevant and accessible when it is given.

Someone living relatively independently will need information on benefits, transport, shopping or holidays for instance, whereas someone who relies on more care and support may simply require everyday information from their carers or service providers about a particular day's activities.

> The NHS and Community Care Act 1990 requires social services to consult service users as a part of the Community Care Planning Process and to provide information about service availability. This reinforces previous legislation and underlines the statutory right of people with learning difficulties to be given information.

An HMSO publication, *Development of Services for People with Learning Disabilities* (1991), states that the Government believes in 'the right of people with learning disabilities to be accorded the same respect and dignity as other citizens and to have their own views and wishes respected at all times'. This implies the right to receive information in an accessible format.

It also highlights the need to involve your audience. If you consult people with learning difficulties about what they need to know and how they would prefer to receive information, you will be able to communicate more effectively with them.

The charity People First has done much to promote self-advocacy and to demonstrate that, given adequate help and advice, people with learning difficulties can have a voice in the community and benefit from access to the information they want and need.

USEFUL MEDIA

Media suitable for providing information to people with learning difficulties are in many cases similar to those useful to older people, people who are visually impaired and those with reading problems. Information in print is not necessarily the most appropriate format. Video or audio tape can be much more user-friendly.

However, it is important not to confuse people with learning difficulties with members of other groups who generally have normal adult vocabularies and understanding of life and the world around them. Although the media used to disseminate information to people with learning difficulties may be the same as for other groups, presentation of the content may need to be substantially different.

There is a broad range of ability among people with learning difficulties, as with any group of people. However, most have difficulty reading and writing, may have problems grasping complicated concepts and will generally be unable to absorb large amounts of information at one go.

Repetition of information is important if people with learning difficulties are to remember it. This includes repetition of visual and factual information. For example, a poster and leaflet relating to the same information should strongly resemble each other visually.

People with learning difficulties need to receive carefully designed and carefully targeted information. Thought must be given to the style of presentation, the media used and the best method of distribution or dissemination.

General rules for supplying information include:

■ Keep it short.

■ Be clear in your own mind what you want to say and why.

■ Ensure that information will be of value to people with learning difficulties.

■ Remember that carers and support services can be useful conduits of information.

■ Always try to test the effectiveness of your information material on people with learning difficulties to check it really does work.

Use of language

54

You should always present your information as clearly and as simply as possible. The guidelines on using plain language will help you achieve this.

When preparing your text remember:

■ Don't use long sentences.

■ Include one main point, and only one or two clauses in a sentence.

■ Write in the active voice, rather than the passive.

■ Avoid abstract concepts.

■ Use simple words, without being patronising.

■ Repeat difficult or unfamiliar words.

■ Don't use jargon.

■ Avoid abbreviations and acronyms.

■ Avoid using the third person – addressing your audience as 'you' is much more user-friendly.

Design

When designing your document it is important to follow certain basic rules:

- Keep line length short.

- Range text left with a ragged right hand margin.

- Use short, clearly separated chunks of text.

- Allow enough space between columns of text.

- Avoid design features which impede legibility such as excessive use of capital letters; stretching or condensing text to fit a particular space; or ornate type faces.

Handwriting is particularly difficult to read for people with learning difficulties. If using the written word is your only option, then ensure it is printed or at least typed.

Illustrations

Pictorial material can help people understand and remember the meaning of the written word. Use illustrations, cartoons, diagrams or photographs to supplement text.

Symbols/Makaton

Symbol systems can help overcome language and communication barriers and help clarify key points in a text. There are several pictorial symbol systems which can be used in conjunction with the written word (ideally in large print).

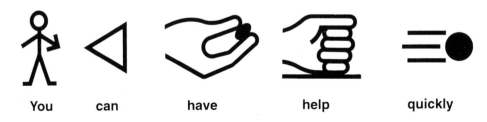

You   **can**   **have**   **help**   **quickly**

Symbols from the Makaton *Patient's Charter*

There is no universally agreed symbol system, but Makaton is perhaps the best known, and can be used in conjunction with other systems such as Blissymbolics and Rebus.

The Makaton system of communication was designed in 1972 by Margaret Walker, a speech and language therapist, and has been adapted for use in over 40 countries. The language has a core vocabulary of around 350 words, signs and symbols for basic needs, and an ever-expanding resource vocabulary – currently around 7000 words.

Makaton assists people with learning difficulties or those who have acquired communication and literacy impairments following an accident, or a stroke perhaps. In recent years the Department of Health has taken an interest in the language and has funded various Makaton projects, including a Makaton version of *The Patient's Charter*, which received extremely positive feedback from people with learning difficulties and from those responsible for their welfare.

Television and video

80, 82

Television and video are especially useful as they do not require the viewer to be able to read or write and they give visual and audio cues which aid comprehension and memory.

Audio tapes

29, 87

Audio tapes can be useful for similar reasons. For longer tapes it is necessary to break up information with jingles and sound effects to maintain interest.

Multi-media

94

People with learning difficulties are often adept at using computers because the interactive set-up can suit their particular needs. Many day centres and adult education places for people with learning difficulties have computing equipment, so floppy discs, the Internet and CDs can be useful information sources, provided the above guidelines are observed.

99

Compact disc technology

CD-I and CD-ROM can be useful tools because of their interactive nature, but the technology is expensive and at an early stage of development. It would be impractical to recommend widespread use yet. However, there is little doubt that this technology will prove increasingly useful to people with learning difficulties in the future.

TARGETING INFORMATION

The information itself, or notification of its availability, can be supplied in most media as long as you use appropriate language. More specifically it can be targeted:

- through social service offices, benefits offices and local health authorities to the individuals concerned or their carers;

- at homes and sheltered accommodation;

- at carers where these are known;

- through charities such as Mencap and People First to clubs and organisations of and for people with learning difficulties; and

- at readers of magazines such as *Gatepost*, aimed specifically at people with learning difficulties.

PEOPLE WITH SEVERE LEARNING DIFFICULTIES

Lobby groups argue that everyone has a right to accessible information but to achieve this for people with severe learning difficulties requires huge resources. These people may live at home, in residential homes or in hospitals. Many attend social education centres. Generally, those supporting them at home or in the community will be their major sources of information. Where information is delivered orally on a one-to-one basis, you can help the specialist communicator to relay the information effectively by keeping the message simple.

PEOPLE WITH MENTAL ILLNESS

As already mentioned, mental illness should not be confused with learning difficulties (mental handicap). Mental illness covers a multitude of conditions including schizophrenia, dementia, nervous breakdown, manic depression, phobias and neuroses, all of which can be treated with drugs and/or therapy (albeit with varying degrees of success).

Mental illness is very common. Doctors diagnose 6 million people as mentally ill every year and of these about 197,000 are admitted to hospital. Because of the huge range in type and severity of mental illness it is not possible to identify specific media or types of information guaranteed to benefit all the members of this group.

Many people with milder forms of mental illness receive and access information in exactly the same ways as the rest of the population. Others, due to impaired mental faculties (be they temporary or permanent), may find information presented in simple terms easier to access, in which case material aimed at people with learning difficulties may prove useful.

Those people who are severely ill will often be in hospital or some other form of staffed accommodation, in which case their carers, social workers or medical services are likely to be their main sources of information and therefore most effective to target.

The type of information generally perceived to be lacking for people who are mentally ill is information that is delivered orally (rather than by printed or other media) by members of the health and social services. To remedy this lack of information requires a change within those services rather than a change in how information in general is presented.

Chapter 7

OLDER PEOPLE

Over six million people in Britain are over 70 years old. They constitute over 10 per cent of the population and demographic forecasts indicate this figure will rise. It is estimated that by the year 2020, one in four people in the European Union be over 60.

Older people constitute a huge minority group to consider when defining your audience and planning your information strategies, especially since 50 per cent of disabled people are over 70.

Being elderly is not in itself a hindrance to receiving or accessing information, but there are a number of conditions which tend to occur or worsen with increasing years which do have this effect. Sight, hearing, memory and other mental faculties can all deteriorate with age. For instance, one in seven people over 75 has a registrable sight impairment. Often coupled with decreased mobility, these impairments can seriously affect a person's ability to receive information at a time when they may most need it.

USEFUL MEDIA

To a large extent, techniques for supplying information to the other groups also apply to older people. It is advisable to assume most older people have either hearing or sight impairment, or both.

Many are not comfortable with 'technology'. They are less likely to own or be able to operate electronic gadgetry such as video or tape recorders, or computers. Older people also tend to have lower incomes than average, which means they are less likely to own such equipment. However, the number of older people discouraged by such gadgetry is diminishing as new generations grow up accustomed to the technology.

Printed material

64–79

As many older people have poor eyesight, it is advisable to follow the Informability guidelines for large print design given in

Chapter 10 or those offered by RNIB. Paying attention to type size, legibility, layout and use of colour will help ensure that your text is accessible to as wide an audience as possible.

Many older people express a preference for simultaneous delivery of oral and written information. (Indeed, research shows oral and written information supplied together is also more effective for younger people.)

Some older people find print difficult to access due to conditions such as arthritis, muscular weakness or tremors which affect their ability to hold or turn the pages of a print document.

Non-print media

The use of media other than print should take account of the particular needs and habits of older people. For instance, they are likely to stop listening to television or radio earlier in the evening than the rest of the population, and may be intimidated by the technology involved in accessing special services such as BBC Focus. Audio cassettes can be useful to older people with visual impairment, but many older people may not have the equipment necessary to play them.

82

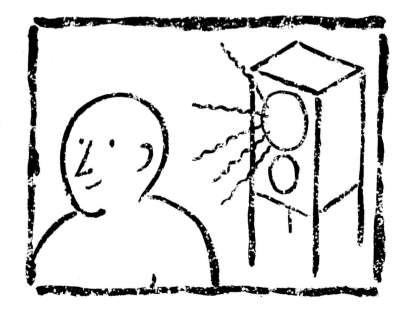

85, 87

For some people, teletext and viewdata services can be helpful. Teletext is especially useful as it is accessible through a domestic television set, can be viewed at leisure and re-referred to if necessary.

102

Telephone response lines

Just under 90 per cent of senior citizens have their own telephone and 97.6 per cent have access to one. This widespread access is encouraging for campaigns offering further information in response to a phone call and is especially useful for people who are housebound.

Where telephone response is encouraged, a textphone number will assist those older people with hearing problems who have access to a textphone.

TARGETING INFORMATION

Older people are less likely to pick up information casually. It is therefore important to target individuals themselves, at old people's homes and sheltered accommodation, or at distribution points from which they are likely to receive it – doctors' surgeries, social services offices, benefits offices, drop-in centres, post offices, supermarkets, national and local charities, etc.

It is also reasonable to assume that older people are more likely to be housebound and therefore rely on media delivered to them. This could be through the front door, via TV or radio, by carers or welfare workers, or other visitors.

Chapter 8

USING PLAIN LANGUAGE

Delivering all your communications in plain language is the single most important step you can take towards making your information accessible to the widest possible audience.

Gobbledegook is rubbish. In other words: a waste of paper, and a waste of time for those who produce it and for those on whose desks or doormats it lands.

In this manual we use the expression 'plain language' in preference to 'plain English' simply because the reasons for writing clearly and plainly apply whatever language you're writing in. Many texts and experts, however, use the phrase 'plain English' and generally speaking the two are interchangeable.

What is plain language?

Martin Cutts, author of *The Plain English Guide* (Oxford University Press 1995) and early pioneer of the use of plain English, describes it as 'the writing and setting out of essential information in a way that gives a co-operative, motivated person a good chance of understanding the document at first reading, and in the same sense that the writer meant it to be understood'.

This description may be a little verbose when measured against Cutts' own recommendations on how to write in plain English, but it also illustrates the fact that your writing should be appropriate to your audience. Plain language does not mean using 'baby talk' or slavishly following guidelines which recommend avoiding long words and long sentences.

The aim is to make sure your message is understood and that it is impossible for it to be misunderstood.

Above all, plain language should be used to disseminate the truth; it should not been seen as an excuse for obscuring or avoiding difficult or unpalatable issues.

Why use plain language?

Using language that everyone can understand benefits not only the information receiver, but also the giver.

The information receiver benefits if you provide information in a user-friendly form. They are more likely to:

■ bother to read a clear, concise document than a complicated, long one;

■ understand what it says;

■ favour companies or organisations which explain things clearly.

You, the information provider, benefit from using plain language because:

■ your message is more likely to be understood and acted upon;

■ it enhances your organisation's profile;

■ avoiding unnecessary enquiries or errors in, for instance, form filling saves staff time and money;

■ shorter documents need less paper, less expense and less storage space.

Supporters of plain language

Traditionally, certain types of messages have been written in the language of the giver even when it has been inappropriate to the receiver. Legal documents, insurance contracts, rules governing benefit claims and so on are obvious examples.

Today, the trend is towards shorter, clearer documents. Much of the credit for this must go to organisations such as the Plain English Campaign (PEC), and the Plain Language Commission (PLC). Both have campaigned for years for public and private bodies to clean up their language.

They also offer advice, help and training to those who want to improve their communication skills.

Both organisations grant marks of accreditation to documents which meet their exacting standards (the Crystal Mark from PEC, and the Clear English Standard from PLC).

Declared supporters of the use of plain language include the Princess Royal, the Princess of Wales, John Major and Margaret Thatcher to name but a few.

In 1982, the British government issued a White Paper requiring government departments to examine their forms and to rewrite or scrap those that didn't work effectively.

The government-backed Better English Campaign seeks to raise awareness of the importance of accurate and effective communication to success at work and in other every-day situations. It also promotes enjoyment of the English language for its own sake.

In the US, Presidents Carter and Clinton have supported moves towards using plain language.

In Italy, the government has commissioned a major project to research and write a code of style (*Codice di Stile*) to help simplify bureaucratic language throughout government.

And European directive 93/13 from the EC Council states:

'In the case of contracts where all or certain terms offered to the consumer are in writing, these terms must always be drafted in plain, intelligible language. Where there is doubt about the meaning of a term, the interpretation most favourable to the consumer shall prevail.'

Objections to plain language

Critics of the use of plain language argue that it is:

- baby talk and so debases the language;

- less precise; and

- not proven to be effective.

51

But these criticisms are simply not justified.

- Plain language guidelines do not preclude the use of appropriate 'adult' language or concepts.

- Testing has shown that putting even legal and complex contractual documents into plain language can make them much less ambiguous and easier to understand by *all* concerned.

- Plain language documents have been widely tested and have proved to benefit a wide spectrum of people, not just those who might be considered the 'lowest common denominator'.

Research

Research confirms that plain language improves comprehension and therefore saves time and money for all concerned.
For example:

In the UK:

- Martin Cutts tested 90 senior law students on a rewritten timeshare law. On one question 94 per cent got the correct answer using the plain English version, compared to 48 per cent when using the original version.

- When Rank Xerox reduced its standard contract from 1,976 words to 176 words in plain English the new contract received a 97.3 per cent approval rating from customers. The company attributed an increase in new and repeat customers directly to the new no-nonsense contract.

In the US:

- A redesigned plain English tax form led to a 450 per cent improvement in comprehension, with 50 per cent of people correctly completing the form in contrast to 10 per cent for the original version.

- Tests on a medical consent form led to a 91 per cent improvement in correctly answered questions.

In Australia:

- Research by the Law Commission among lawyers and law students showed that the time needed to read and comprehend legal statutes was reduced by between one-third and a half when statutes were written in plain language.

Text for translation

3, 10

In our increasingly multilingual society, many documents need to be translated – into the many ethnic languages commonly used in the UK, and into the various languages of the European Union member states.

If the original document is written in plain language, then the translator's work will be easier and the translation is more likely to be accurate.

This saves money and time, and leads to less potential misunderstanding.

Plain language guidelines

There are a number of guidelines, recognised by most champions of plain language, which will help you write clearly and succinctly. However, the guidelines are not prescriptive. Good writing is largely a matter of practice and common sense.

Many organisations already have style guidelines on how to write clear, effective documents. The Benefits Agency, for instance, offers advice to its staff on how to write letters to clients and also has a Document Design Unit dedicated to simplifying forms and other documents for use by the public. And Kirklees Metropolitan Council publishes guidance for its employees on plain language and clear print.

We have based the Informability guidelines on our own experience in the field, on advice given by the various plain language organisations and on codes of style produced by others interested in making their information more generally accessible.

*inform*ability
PLAIN LANGUAGE GUIDELINES

Thinking before inking

Do you know what you're doing? Before you prepare your text consider whether you've chosen the most appropriate format. A personalised letter may be more appropriate than a newspaper advert – and possibly cheaper. Or a poster may be more likely to be seen and read than a lengthy leaflet. The format will affect the content and style of your writing.

To make your documents clear and precise, you need to be clear in your own mind:

- who you are addressing;

- what you want to tell them;

- what they want and need to know; and

- what you want them to do as a result.

Take time to plan your text:

- Decide what you want to say and in what order. For instance, this may mean putting the points in order of importance, or in the order in which instructions should be carried out.

- Think about the language with which your audience is likely to be familiar or unfamiliar.

- Weed out inessential or irrelevant information.

Planning the structure

- Summarise the key points of the document at the beginning.

- Start with the most important information your reader needs to know.

- Use clear headings to break up the text, even in short documents.

- Provide navigational aids to steer the reader through the text. These could include:

- a contents list;

- informative headings;

- boxed or highlighted text for emphasis;

- lists, tables or bullet points rather than long sentences;

- running headers.

- If some technical words or jargon are unavoidable, think about including a glossary.

Style guidelines

Tom Vernon wrote in *Gobbledegook* in 1980 'Write as if you are speaking to somebody on the other side of the desk, and as if that person was somebody you would like to become your friend.' The following guidelines will help you to achieve this.

- Use language your audience will understand.

- Split your information into short, easily absorbed paragraphs or sections.

- Keep sentences short – an average of 15–20 words throughout the text.

- Don't include too many ideas in a sentence. One main idea, with possibly one sub-clause, is enough for most sentences.

- Be as brief as you can without losing clarity. The clearest word order is subject, verb, object.

- Avoid abbreviations. If you do need to use abbreviations, write the words in full the first time you use them, followed by the abbreviation in brackets.

- Avoid jargon. Choose simple, everyday words in preference to bureaucratic, technical, old-fashioned or flowery language.

- When you have to use particular words for the sake of accuracy, explain them in plain language the first time you use them.

- Keep punctuation simple and accurate. Many people are confused by semi-colons, colons, square brackets etc. Many more are confused by sloppy or ambiguous use of punctuation.

- Be direct. People respond more positively to a direct style. For example, don't be afraid to write in the first person or to address the reader as 'you': 'We will tell you if . . . '; or 'I received your letter about . . . '.

- Write in the active, rather than passive voice: 'we will write to you ', rather than 'a letter will be sent'; 'we will decide', rather than 'a decision will be made'. Passive verbs are all too common in bureaucratic writing.

- Repeat words rather than use alternatives simply for the sake of variety. For instance, it would be confusing to use 'client', 'customer', 'passenger' and 'ticket holder' in the same document if they all mean the same thing.

- Avoid ambiguity. Ambiguity could include:

- words or sentences with more than one meaning;

- words such as 'it', 'this', 'they' which refer back to something you have already mentioned;

- words which have different meanings in different contexts.

- Avoid negatives. 'Please return the form by 1 April 1997' is friendlier and easier to understand than 'We will not be able to deal with forms returned after 1 April 1997'.

- Avoid using phrases where a single verb will do. Use:

- 'apply' rather than 'make an application';

- 'deliver' rather than 'arrange a delivery to';

- 'decide' rather than 'make a decision'.

- Avoid cross references. Repetition (within reason) is clearer.

Be flexible

The guidelines for writing plain language are simply guidelines. They are not rigid rules which have to be followed no matter what. There will always be occasions when it is more appropriate to ignore or adjust the guidelines.

- Sentences over 20 words are not banned. Although sentences should never be too long, varying their length can result in a less abrupt effect, and a more readable style.

- There is also no harm in breaking the traditional rules of grammar if it makes the sense clearer:

- you can end a sentence with a preposition; be guided by common usage; for instance 'the people you talk to' sounds more natural than 'the people to whom you talk';

- there is also no harm in starting sentences with 'And', 'But' or 'Because' if it helps to split a long sentence into two more manageable ones.

- If your text is for experts in a particular field, then by all means use the technical terms your readers will be familiar with.

Language should be flexible, so should plain language guidelines.

Warning!

Beware of relying too much on computers to check your writing. Although some programs can give you a quick overall assessment of certain aspects of your writing, they cannot tell you if your writing is good or not. Readability formulae, spell-checks and grammar-checks can never replace someone else reading your text. Nor can technology spot all the mistakes, as anyone who's ever put too much faith in a spell-check will know.

Chapter 9

MAKING ALL YOUR INFORMATION ACCESSIBLE

There is no simple answer to the question 'Which are the most effective media for getting a message to the largest number of people?'. This is because it is not usually possible to class any one group as more important or more deserving than any other.

Ideally, information should be available in a variety of formats so that users can select the one which best suits their own needs. This is the goal which lobby groups strive to persuade information providers to achieve.

Many of the media useful for making information accessible to the groups described in the preceding chapters are those used to target the population in general: e.g. print, TV, radio. Others are more specialised: e.g. braille, audio tape, BSL signed video.

There is often a temptation to cut corners when producing material in alternative formats on the assumption that anything is better than nothing. This approach can be counter-productive as it may reinforce the audience's opinion that it is, as usual, being offered second class treatment.

All information providers, whatever media they chose to use, should bear in mind certain basic rules:

- Keep language straightforward – whether it is spoken or printed.

- Don't patronise your audience.

- Consider layout, design and typography in relation to your audience.

- Ensure that information in alternative formats is well publicised and easy to obtain.

- Try to ensure that alternative formats are made available at the same time as the standard print version.

- Subtitle all video (preferably in a 'closed' form).

- Wherever possible give a telephone number in publicity material, and a textphone number.

- Consult your audience as to their needs and preferences.

Consultation

One of the most important aspects of providing information for particular audiences is consultation. It is much better to consult your audience about their needs than to assume you know what's best for them in any given situation.

Encourage your customers to let you know what their information preferences and needs are, and keep a record of their responses. This will help you build up an overall picture of the audience as well as keeping you up-to-date with individuals' specific needs.

You may also find that if you bother to ask them, your customers may be able to give advice on improving your services – not simply by requesting more information in accessible media, but also by giving an informed view on efficient processes and by identifying potential savings.

Prioritising your information

Although you should try to provide a multi-format service, economically it is not always possible to achieve this. Inevitably, it may be necessary for you to identify the types of information to which you need to give priority.

RNIB recommends that priority is given to essential or 'citizen' information, which they define as:

- information needed to exercise the rights and responsibilities of citizenship, for example, voting or paying taxes;

- information of a personal or confidential nature, especially financial and medical matters, such as bills, bank statements and medical details;

- information from which legal consequences may result if not acted upon, such as a court summons.

Although RNIB makes its recommendations in specific relation to blind and partially sighted people, the principles can equally well be applied to information provision to the other groups covered in this manual.

The Informability Unit agrees in principle with these categories, but prefers to define the priorities more broadly to include:

- All information aimed at a general audience.

- Any information directly applicable to a particular audience, e.g. relating to disability.

Publicising alternative formats

One of the problems for many people – not just those with disabilities or literacy difficulties – is that they don't know what information may be available. Having produced alternative formats, it's no good simply sitting back and waiting for results.

In order to ensure the effectiveness of your information strategies you must publicise the existence and means of getting hold of the alternative formats.

- The simplest and most economical way is to make sure that you mention the other formats in standard print material and catalogues. Although your audiences may not find this information accessible, they may pick up information from others who do use standard print.

- Mention all formats in all media versions. Thus, the braille version of a leaflet should also mention the standard print, large print, audio cassette and BSL video versions for example, and how to get hold of copies. This is simple enough to achieve if given thought at the planning stage.

- Inviting responses to a direct mail shot or coupon can help you avoid producing more copies than are required by accurately establishing your potential audience in advance.

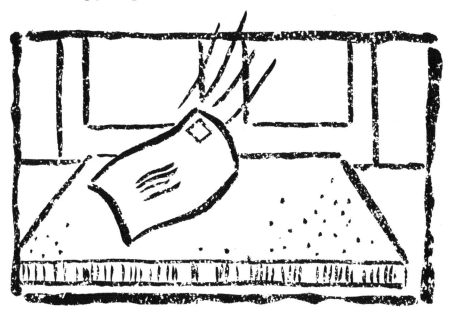

- Local radio is a powerful medium, especially among people with a visual impairment, about a third of whom listen to it regularly. Some stations broadcast programmes specially for people with disabilities.

- Whenever possible, try to get some editorial coverage in publications likely to be interested in either the subject matter or the very fact that it is available in accessible media.

- Most public libraries stock information in forms other than standard print. Many have large print and audio cassette sections; some offer videos, CDs and access to the Internet. Others run mobile services which reach wider audiences. The *Share the Vision* project promotes the development of services in libraries for people with visual impairment.

- Many national and local organisations concerned with literacy or disability offer distribution services for information material in accessible formats or can provide publicity for the information among their particular audiences.

- Remember also to mention accessible formats at the press launch of any campaign or publication.

When planning how to target your information, it is also important to remember that most disabled people read the same publications, watch the same TV programmes, visit the same places as everyone else, and that their appreciation of quality is no different from other people's.

So it would be a mistake to assume that by placing information within a disability magazine, for example, you will effectively reach the majority of people who are disabled. National newspapers and publications such as *Radio Times, Woman's Own* or *Hello!* may be more effective because they have large circulations, and many of their readers belong to the groups described in this manual.

Also most people with disabilities visit the supermarket or post office more regularly than, for instance, their GP's surgery. For a distribution point to be effective it does not necessarily have to be connected with disability or claiming benefits.

ACCESSIBLE MEDIA

Chapters 10–14 describe the following media and their potential usefulness to the audiences dealt with in previous chapters:

Chapter 10: Print media

- Standard print
- Large print
- Braille (and Moon)

Chapter 11: Broadcast media

- Television
- Video
- Subtitling
- Audio description
- Teletext
- Viewdata
- Audio tape
- Radio

Chapter 12: Multi-media

- Information on disc
- The Internet
- Compact disc technology

Chapter 13: Telephones and helplines

- Textphones and Typetalk
- Videophones

Chapter 14: Signage

- Visual signs
- Tactile signs
- Audible Signs
- Signs of the future

Chapter 10

PRINT MEDIA

11, 25

STANDARD PRINT

Printed text intended for a general audience is usually between 8pt and 10pt in size and generally no bigger than 12pt. This manual, for instance, is set in 12pt Century Book.

Standard print includes information in any printed newspaper or magazine, either as editorial or as paid advertising. It also includes anything printed in books, specialist publications, booklets or leaflets.

The written word, after the spoken word, is the oldest and most widely used method of communication. Text in print form therefore tends to be the most popular medium with information providers. It is not, however, always the most efficient or accessible medium for many people, including some who can read. Much depends on the type of message involved, the audience, and whether the information is for immediate use or for storage and retrieval later.

> All print intended to inform, whatever type size, should always be as clear and as legible as possible.

It is also important that your writing and editorial style ensure that the text can be understood by a wide audience but is not off-putting to the majority of readers because of over-simplistic use of language or design.

Distribution of standard print

Distribution networks are usually already well established for standard print. Printed material should always contain details of information available in other formats.

Accessibility of standard print

People with literacy problems
Not fully accessible to many. The guidelines on plain language
in Chapter 8 will help you to prepare text which will maximise
understanding by this audience.

Prelingually Deaf
Not accessible to many of the prelingually Deaf community due to
low levels of literacy.

Hard of hearing
Accessible to the majority of people who are hard of hearing
or have become deaf after learning to read.

Blind
Not accessible to the majority unless they have access
to sophisticated technological aids.

Partially sighted
Accessible to around 60 per cent of partially sighted people,
although it is rarely the preferred medium and may only be useful
for imparting small amounts of information, provided care is taken
over design and print quality.

Deaf-blind
Not accessible to the vast majority.

People with learning difficulties
Not accessible to many. To maximise understanding, you should
follow the guidelines on layout, design and use of language in
Chapter 6.

Older people
Not accessible to some, due to sight impairment or physical
disablement.

65

25

LARGE PRINT

There is currently some debate over the use of the terms 'large print' and 'clear print'. To be effective, all print should be 'clear', whatever its size. We have used the term 'large print' in this manual to mean 14pt type and above. This is the minimum size you should use for a document for people with a visual impairment.

RNIB recommends 'a clear print standard' of 12pt type for a general audience; and a minimum of 14pt for blind and partially sighted readers. There appears to be no advantage in enlarging type above about 20pt (except for headings). Your choice of point size will depend on your subject matter and your audience.

But size is not everything. It is also important to take typeface, type weight, line length, leading (space between lines), layout and print quality into account when designing for large print.

Large print is not simply standard print made larger.

Unfortunately, no one design style will suit everybody. Different eye conditions have different effects on how the eye functions. However, if you take guidelines on large print design into account you will make your documents accessible to a much larger audience.

The Informability Unit has its own guidelines for print design for blind and partially sighted readers. The guidelines are used by COI's own designers, who helped to compile them.

The guidelines provide a framework within which to work, but the most important thing is to consider the difficulties visually impaired people encounter and how these can be alleviated by sensible design. Most of the guidelines are simply a matter of common sense.

RNIB also publishes guidelines on the design of material in large print.

*inform*ability
LARGE PRINT GUIDELINES

typeface
Always use clear text faces and avoid bizarre, indistinct or ornate faces. (The typeface we have used for these guidelines is 14pt Century Book with 3pt leading.)

type size
A minimum size of 14pt is recommended for people with a visual impairment. Take account of the appearing size of the face (some faces appear larger than others at the same point size). Consider reducing the volume of copy before reducing the type size.

type weight
Use a medium or bold weight and avoid light faces, especially in smaller type sizes.

type style
Avoid italics and excessive use of capital letters as these letterforms affect the outline shape of words and are therefore more difficult to read.

reversing out
Only reverse type out of a background colour if the face is clear, bold enough and large enough not to break up or fill in with ink. Ensure a good contrast between white lettering and the background colour.

leading
Allow adequate leading (the space between lines of type). Minimum 2pt leading for 12pt, more for larger sizes.

letter spacing

Ensure adequate, even spacing between letters. Letters should never appear to touch.

word spacing

Keep word spacing even. Don't condense or stretch lines of type to fit a particular measure.

line length

Allow 50–65 characters, inclusive of spaces, per line. Less than 65 is preferable and text set in columns may well have less than 50 characters per line.

justification

Ranged left type with a ragged right hand margin is easier to read than justified type.

hyphenation

Don't split words at the end of lines – i.e. avoid hyphenation.

layout

Keep layout clean and logical. Provide contents lists and plenty of clear headings to act as signposts for the reader. Break text into shortish paragraphs with adequate space between and around them.

columns

Allow adequate space between columns. Use rules to separate columns if they must be close together. It is not a good idea to use designs with uneven column widths.

pictorial material

Do not run type over or around illustrations/photos etc. Use bold images if using images at all.

form design

Remember that people with a visual impairment often have large handwriting and need more space in which to write. Text and related boxes for writing or putting a tick in should be clearly associated with each other. A large gap can cause confusion or errors.

contrast/colour

Contrast between background and type is crucial for legibility. Black on white or yellow is best for most people. Always use dark colours on light. Remember colour blindness: 1 in 12 men and 1 in 200 women can't distinguish between red and green.

paper

Use matt papers. Glossy surfaces can create glare. Avoid thin or semi-transparent papers which allow show-through.

Fine tuning

There are many other aspects of typography which can affect legibility. For instance:

- Whether the typeface is serif or sanserif. Younger people tend to prefer sanserif faces, older people tend to prefer serif faces.

- The length of ascenders (b, d, f, h, k, l, t) and descenders (g, j, p, q, y) in relation to the x-height of the typeface. Short ascenders and descenders tend to make a typeface less legible.

- The individual characteristics of letter shapes. For instance, a closed 'ɑ' is more likely to be confused with a 'c' or an 'o' than an open 'a' is; a 3 can be confused with an 8 in some typefaces.

- Stress – the relative thickness and thinness of the strokes which make up the letterform. Strongly stressed typefaces are less legible than faces with more even stroke widths.

J.H. Prince PhD, in an article for *The Journal of Typographic Research* in 1967, even goes so far as to say: 'Periods [full stops] and commas need to be enlarged beyond present sizes . . . [This] is voluntarily and persistently commented upon by large numbers of both normal – and subnormal – vision subjects used in reading tests.'

Once we overlook Dr Prince's rather insensitive use of language, his recommendation sounds very logical, yet modern designers for visually impaired audiences don't seem to have adapted their punctuation marks so far.

I mention Dr Prince's recommendation simply as an example of how much scope there is for development of good practice where design for large print is concerned.

Things to avoid

Large print is accessible, albeit not necessarily ideal, to virtually anyone who can read standard print. However, for people with average eyesight, type is most legible when it is of a particular size and read at a particular distance. So large print, although not impossible to read for the majority audience, can have an off-putting effect. It may also be seen to suggest a disabled or illiterate target audience with which some people may not wish to be identified.

When designing for large print you should try to avoid making the document look as if it's aimed at children – the 'Janet and John' design style.

It is also better to use standard page sizes for large print documents. Although it may seem logical to use a larger page size, this is not recommended. Large documents are awkward to handle and won't fit on standard bookshelves or in filing cabinets. And most people prefer not to be made to feel conspicuously different. You should therefore try to avoid supplying your information in conspicuously different formats.

Desk-top publishing

When you only need one or a small number of copies of a document, it is often possible to produce them using desk-top publishing. However, when laying out the document you should still follow the guidelines for designing for large print.

. . . but beware!

Beware the typographic default settings of software. For instance, many default settings position letters and words too closely together; use inappropriate hyphenation and inadequate line spacing. Even on the office wordprocessor you may like to change the default settings so that you automatically produce all your documents in a suitably legible format.

Distribution of large print

Large print can be distributed to much the same outlets as standard print since it is accessible to so many people. Specific targeting at and through organisations dealing with visual impairment is also recommended.

The availability of large print should also be flagged up in standard print and any other versions of the document.

Accessibility of large print

People with literacy problems
Not accessible to many, although large print may be beneficial provided layout and language are uncomplicated.

Prelingually Deaf
No more accessible than standard print to the majority of the Deaf community.

Hard of hearing
Accessible to most, including many older people with visual as well as hearing impairment.

Blind
Potentially accessible to 36 per cent of people who are blind but regularly used by only 12 per cent.

Partially sighted
Potentially accessible to the 75 per cent of people with visual impairment who have enough sight to read large print (although not necessarily with ease) but commonly used by only 29 per cent.

Deaf-blind
Accessible to a few of those with some sight.

People with learning difficulties
Not accessible to many, although large print may be beneficial if layout and language are uncomplicated. Large type in conjunction with symbols can also increase accessibility.

Older people
Accessible to a large number of older people with visual impairment.

26

BRAILLE

Braille is an important medium because it allows perusal and retention of information and ease of reference for braille users.

Despite the relatively small number of people able to read braille – only 2 per cent of the visually impaired population – its importance as an efficient medium for distributing information should not be underestimated, as the 22 per cent of blind people between 16 and 59 years old who use it often occupy influential positions. It is most commonly used by younger people.

What is braille?

Braille is a system of raised dots that can be read by touch. It uses patterns of up to six dots to represent each letter or number.

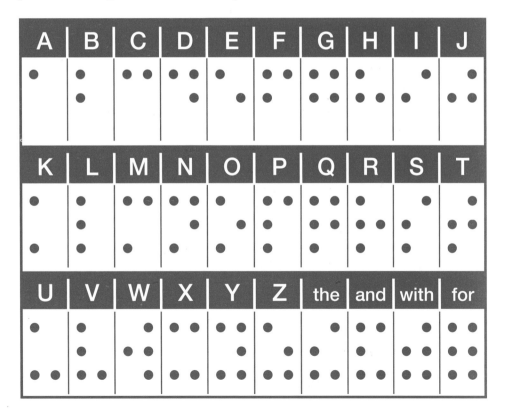

Braille letters are formed by a combination of raised dots. Devised by a Frenchman, the original alphabet had no W.

Types of braille

There are two types of English braille.

Grade one is a straightforward letter-by-letter transcription.

Grade two is a condensed version where common words and letter sequences are abbreviated.

It is generally best to produce documents in Grade two braille as it is the form used by experienced braille readers who form the majority of the audience.

Grade two is also:

- shorter;
- quicker to read;
- less bulky; and
- cheaper to produce.

However, it will not be perfectly understood by less adept readers.

Preparing text for brailling

Text for reproduction as braille can be re-keyed or scanned onto a computer from hard copy. Ideally, however, text should be supplied to the braille transcriber on floppy disc or by other electronic means. This saves time and money and reduces the possibility of error.

You may also need to edit your text. With a little common sense it isn't difficult to spot parts of the text which need adapting for braille readers. However, conversion of visual elements such as tables or diagrams into a braille equivalent, or into narrative text, are skilled processes best done by the professionals.

There are various conventions governing the layout of braille documents. These cover such considerations as:

- positioning and hierarchy of headings;
- addition of a contents list;
- use of running headings;
- use of indentations;
- layout of tables;
- page numbering: both of the braille pages and with reference to those in the print version – the print page indicator (PPI).

For bulk publishing, always use specialist braille producers. But even when dealing with experts, you should emphasise the importance of high standards of production.

Design of covers for braille documents

Obviously, the cover of a braille document should bear the title and possibly other information such as a subtitle, author's or publisher's name in braille.

Although most braille users are unlikely to take much interest in the aesthetic appearance of the cover, there are also good reasons for giving the design some thought.

Using a bold design printed in strong colour(s) will:

- help braille users who have some useful sight to identify the document quickly on the shelf;

- help non-braille users who handle the document (people responsible for fulfilment mailing for instance) to identify the document;

- link the document visually to others related to it in braille or other formats.

Short print runs

For small-scale production – such as letters, bills or short print runs – automatic translation software enables non-braille users to produce braille documents reasonably effectively from standard wordprocessed copy on disc.

However, it is worth getting an experienced braille reader to check that your software and braille transcriber are producing reasonable quality braille. Some software may use an inappropriate system – an American version for instance or one that is out of date.

The conventions covering standard braille contractions can alter with changing demand and new software. It is important therefore that braille transcribers keep up to date with the latest conventions and transcription software.

Organisations with in-house transcription facilities need to be alert to the fact that old software programs may no longer produce the most accessible transcriptions.

Notice of Intention to Transcribe

RNIB keeps a register of documents which have been transcribed into braille. This record includes RNIB's own output and details of documents produced by other transcribers. It is intended to help braille users and transcribers to save time and money by avoiding duplication.

The system only works, of course, as long as braille producers supply RNIB with a 'Notice of Intention to Transcribe' each time they plan to produce a new braille document.

Disadvantages of braille

Braille can present certain problems. Braille is:

- inaccessible to anyone not skilled in its use – this makes errors difficult to spot for sighted information providers;

- bulky – braille paper is thick and heavy, and braille occupies around three times as much area as typescript; its weight makes bulk storage difficult because the raised dots can become compressed and therefore illegible;

- relatively expensive to produce – but, as with print, the unit cost reduces as the print run lengthens and set-up costs are spread more thinly.

Distribution of braille

You should make braille available through organisations dealing with visual impairment, or target it directly at braille users. The availability of braille should also be flagged up in other media and details given on how to obtain it. Where demand is anticipated to be slight, braille can be supplied in response to individual requests from a small stock (which can be replenished if necessary).

 32

Braille can be sent free of charge by first class post using the Royal Mail's Articles for the Blind service.

Accessibility of braille

People with literacy problems
Not accessible.

Prelingually Deaf
Not accessible.

Hard of hearing
Not accessible.

Blind
Actively used by 13,000 people who are blind. It can be understood by a further 6,000 who can read braille but prefer to use other media, and by many others who are not fluent but can make use of braille labelling and signposting for example.

Partially sighted
Not generally accessible except for limited use on packaging, lift buttons etc.

Deaf-blind
One of only three media potentially accessible to people who are severely deaf-blind (the others being Moon and manual signing). However, by no means all deaf-blind people read braille.

People with learning difficulties
Not accessible.

Older people
Not accessible.

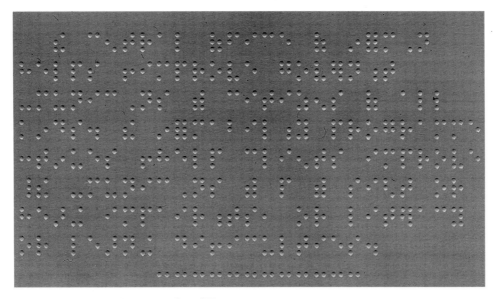

A page of grade two braille.

28

MOON

Moon is read by so few people (around 1,000) that it can generally be ignored by most information providers.

It is difficult and expensive to produce and although RNIB, for instance, aims to communicate in a person's preferred medium and will transcribe documents into Moon if asked, it does not encourage requests for this service. It does, however, publish a Moon Teaching Pack and several magazines (none of which has a circulation of more than 300–400).

Chapter 11

BROADCAST MEDIA

20, 28

TELEVISION

Ninety-eight per cent of households have a colour television and 69 per cent a video recorder. Average viewing per head of population is around 24 hours a week, so broadcast television is a major source of information for the vast majority of the population, and a popular source of information for older people and people with literacy problems. It can also be specially adapted to reach a number of other groups such as deaf and hard of hearing and even visually impaired people.

Television/video is the only medium with widespread access which allows the use of BSL and is therefore accessible to Deaf audiences. (Some new media such as CD-I can also deliver moving images, but they are much less commonly available.)

Most deaf and hard of hearing people people have televisions, and access to teletext is considerably higher among people with hearing impairment than it is for the population in general.

However, although television is popular with viewers, it is an expensive medium for information providers.

Accessibility of Television

People with literacy problems
Accessible. Television is a major source of information.

Prelingually Deaf
Not accessible unless signed translation and/or signing presenters are used.

Hard of hearing
Can be accessible to those who have difficulty understanding speech on television, provided subtitles (open or closed) are included, and the viewer has the technology to access them. Some people who are hard of hearing have induction loop systems linked to their TVs which help them to hear the sound track.

Blind
Can be accessible. Sixty per cent of people with visual impairment rate television as their most important source of information. Many 'watch' television and receive information provided the message does not rely heavily on visual images and the sound-track carries the necessary information, or audio description is provided.

Partially sighted
Can be accessible (see Blind).

Deaf-blind
Can be accessible to some if presented in BSL, and/or the sound-track is clear and comprehensive.

People with learning difficulties
Can be accessible provided the message is presented simply.

Older people
Generally accessible, although less so to the high proportion of people with visual and hearing impairment. Television is a major source of information, especially to those who are housebound or have mobility difficulties.

BBC Focus

BBC Focus is a special television service broadcast between 4a.m. and 6a.m. as part of the BBC's Learning Zone service. It provides non-profit-making organisations such as charities with the opportunity to become involved in making their own television programmes to communicate specialist information, education or training material to their particular audiences. The programmes are intended for video recording and viewing at a more convenient time.

20, 22, 28

VIDEO

Video is accessible to similar audiences to television. And as with television, video can be useful both for making information more easily understood and in targeting that information efficiently. It can be subtitled to assist people with hearing impairment, include BSL for Deaf people, or carry audio description for those with visual impairment. Video does not depend on high levels of literacy in its audiences.

Video incorporating BSL is especially effective for targeting the Deaf community because tapes can be selectively distributed to appropriate television programmes, deaf publications, clubs, charities, schools etc, to ensure that they are seen by as many of the target audience as possible.

Video can also be used to target people who are deaf-blind and those with learning difficulties provided the particular needs of the audiences are catered for.

21

SUBTITLING

Subtitling is generally used to make television or video accessible to people who are deaf or hard of hearing. Most people in these groups have access to a television despite around 4.2 million people having difficulty understanding speech on the television. Subtitling can be added quickly and relatively cheaply to new or existing material and assists as many as 2.4 million people to understand speech on the television.

An estimated 97 per cent of deaf and hard of hearing households have teletext which carries subtitling on page 888.

Subtitling can be either 'open' or 'closed'. Open subtitling appears on the screen automatically, so all viewers are obliged to see it. Closed subtitling, such as teletext, allows the viewer to choose to access subtitles or not. Some commercial videos also carry closed captioning. This is accessed using a decoder.

There are currently (1996) over 100 hours of teletext subtitling on BBC1 and BBC2 combined per week, including 26 hours of live programmes; 54 hours on ITV; and over 76 hours on Channel 4. These hours are increasing annually because the 1990 Broadcasting Act requires 50 per cent of ITV output to be subtitled by 1998. Channel 4 has already achieved 50 per cent coverage and the BBC has pledged to match this figure.

With this deadline in mind, it is arguable that all information providers should ensure that they include subtitling via teletext on any material intended for broadcast. This would enable many more people who are deaf or hard of hearing to access televised information without disturbing other viewers.

It is indicative of American advertisers' keenness to reach a wider audience that around 90 per cent of US commercials are subtitled.

You should always pay attention to the legibility of subtitles. Their effectiveness depends on the size of the lettering, their position on the screen and the contrast with the background.

There are also Independent Television Commission (ITC) rules on how subtitles may be used and what information they can and should contain.

28

AUDIO DESCRIPTION

Audio description is an additional narration which fits between dialogue and gives extra descriptive information that helps visually impaired viewers to follow visual action such as body language, facial expression, changing scenes and so on.

Television, theatre, film and video can all be audio described. On television audio description requires a separate sound channel.

Audio description on television

Audio description was pioneered in the US. In Britain it has been the subject of an EC project – Audetel – funded through TIDE and led by the ITC.

In 1994 the BBC and ITV companies, in conjunction with the RNIB, made a number of pilot programmes to test the system using prototype receivers in the homes of 100 visually impaired viewers.

To receive audio description via the analogue broadcasting system we have at the moment requires a special receiver linked to the television aerial but, in time, the technology could be incorporated into new television sets and video recorders.

With the arrival of digital terrestrial broadcasting Audetel is becoming an even more practical possibility. The government is in favour of developing digital terrestrial services and the broadcasting companies are also committed to implementing the service on digital television.

Audio description on video

Audio description on video requires no special equipment and is already available on some commercial videos. The RNIB runs a home rental service of audio described films and TV programmes for people with visual impairment.

TELETEXT

'Teletext' is the generic term for textual information that can be called up at any time on a television screen (assuming the technology is installed in the set) and examined at leisure.

There are two main UK teletext companies/services – Ceefax (BBC) and Teletext Ltd (ITV). These teletext services are especially useful for supplying updates on current information, making special announcements, or cross-referencing or supplementing other information such as that given in television programmes, fillers or commercials.

Teletext services are accessed by 17 million TV viewers each week and generate over 14 million requests for information. Some 20 per cent of package holidays are reportedly sold through teletext.

The main current objections to using teletext are the difficulties of persuading viewers to use the service for a range of information needs over and above holidays, TV listings, sport and weather; and persuading information providers that the audience will bother to access information if it is supplied. However, people are becoming increasingly familiar with the idea of accessing information from a screen. And the advantage of teletext is that the viewer only requires a domestic TV set, and not a computer, to use the system.

Teletext subtitling to television programmes is accessed through page 888 on both Ceefax and Teletext.

Accessibility of teletext

People with literacy problems
Not generally accessible or favoured.

Prelingually Deaf
Not accessible to the majority of prelingually Deaf people due
to limited literacy in English.

Hard of hearing
Accessible.

Blind
Not accessible unless an audio output facility is available.
It may also be inaccessible to people with certain types of
colour blindness.

Partially sighted
Accessible to some. Much depends on the quality of the text
on the screen.

Deaf-blind
Not accessible.

People with learning difficulties
Not generally accessible.

Older people
Accessible to some. For people who need time to make sense of or
absorb information, and for people who are housebound, teletext
can be extremely useful.

VIEWDATA

Viewdata is a system for accessing information from a central database using telephone lines and a modified television or PC.

Viewdata systems are user-responsive and quick to update. They can be used effectively in meeting local information needs and targeting specific local audiences. Many local authorities operate their own systems with terminals in libraries, shopping malls etc. However, Prestel, the only national carrier, is strongly business-focused and access to the system by the general public is not widespread. Should Prestel become more accessible or suggestions for linking local authority systems come to fruition, Viewdata would be useful for wider dissemination of information.

29, 41

AUDIO TAPE

Audio tape is an especially useful medium for delivering lengthy information which needs to be kept and referred back to. It is accessible to much the same audience as radio and can be useful to people who have difficulty with print for reasons such as visual impairment, reduced manual dexterity, or cerebral palsy. It is also used by people who simply find tape more convenient than print – when driving or doing housework for instance.

Eighty per cent of visually impaired people under 60 and 42 per cent over 60 have cassette tape players, while 12 per cent have an RNIB Talking Books machine which plays the special 8-track tapes (called carts) supplied by the company.

As a general rule, audio tape should be professionally produced, be clear and concise, and use professional voice-overs, music/jingles and sound effects (although dramatic devices should never be allowed to overshadow the tape's message).

If long, tapes can also include tone indexing to allow efficient reference to specific pieces of information. Tone indexing is only useful to people with tape machines equipped to relay audible codes during fast forward and reverse, but does not create barriers to understanding for those without such machines.

Although it is certainly possible to produce audio tapes cheaply this is never worthwhile if you want a large number of copies. Cheap recordings are usually poor quality and on poor stock. Poor sound quality is as bad as poor quality print is for a sighted person; and poor quality stock can damage a tape player.

Sometimes, you may want to produce one-off tapes to provide information quickly and cheaply for individuals – a letter or the minutes of a meeting for instance. On these occasions you should take care that the recording is as clear and as well organised as possible.

As a rough guide, a C60 tape will record approximately 9,000 words and a C90 takes about 12,000. C120s are not generally recommended as longer tapes can be prone to breaking.

Tapes can be useful to a wide cross-section of people, so be careful when labelling them. It is usually better to avoid suggesting that tapes are aimed specifically at 'disabled people'.

The Confederation of Tape Information Services (COTIS) also provides useful guidelines on tape production.

*inform*ability
AUDIO TAPE PRODUCTION GUIDELINES

Designers of printed material use visual elements to help readers find their way around a document and to maintain interest. Tape producers need to provide sound clues for the same purposes.

The following guidelines can help at the planning stage to make your tapes as accessible as possible to their listeners:

- Arrange the information in a logical order for listeners.

- Adapt the written text to create a script suitable for voice(s). For instance, tables and diagrams must be presented in a comprehensible manner.

- Give a summary of the subject and a contents list at the start.

- Number items and use the numbers in the contents list and at the start of each item.

- Place key information such as contact numbers, addresses and key facts and figures at the beginning or end of the side or item so that they are easy to find and to refer back to.

- Tell your listeners what is coming next so that they can decide whether to carry on listening or skip to the next item.

- Separate items clearly with a short silence, piece of music and/or tone indexing.

- Say when the recording or side is ending so the listener knows that the silence is not due to a fault on the tape or the machine.

- Use voices experienced in presenting information on tape and appropriate to the subject matter and audience. For instance, older people tend to prefer slower speech.

- Consider using more than one voice, especially if the text is long as this adds variety and 'colour' to the recording.

- Ensure you make good quality master recordings and duplicates. Poor sound quality is as bad as illegible print.

Distribution of audio tape

A number of organisations provide information services on audio tape. They can sometimes help publicise taped material.

Talking Newspapers, the RNIB and COI, for instance, produce and circulate taped information on a regular basis.

Tape can be used effectively to target particular groups and individuals:

■ by meeting individual requests in response to a publicity campaign or direct mailing;

■ through organisations which have existing tape distribution facilities and themselves provide information on audio tape;

■ through some of the 1,400 charities for people with visual impairment;

■ through clubs and societies for people with visual impairment or learning difficulties;

■ through local or national radio stations which may be prepared to play the whole tape, or flag up its existence; BBC programmes such as *In Touch* and *Does He Take Sugar?* are sometimes glad to receive material they could use in the programmes and/or review for their audiences;

■ in libraries, which nowadays also provide information in forms other than the printed word, including on tape.

Caution is needed when preparing tapes for distribution via the Articles for the Blind postal scheme since rules govern the content – for instance the amount of music which can be included.

Packaging

Whenever possible it is preferable to package audio cassettes in card slip covers rather than plastic boxes. Shattered plastic can be dangerous – especially to someone with a sight impairment – and there is no danger of card covers breaking in the post. Tapes intended for visually impaired audiences should have as large print as space allows on the covers.

Accessibility of audio tape

People with literacy problems
Accessible.

Prelingually Deaf
Not accessible.

Hard of hearing
Generally not accessible.

Blind
Accessible. But audio tape is not a substitute for braille. It is helpful to label tapes in braille, but this is labour-intensive and expensive. If tapes are for a mixed audience, braille should only be applied to tapes for blind readers so not to imply that the information is only 'for blind people'.

Partially sighted
Accessible – see Blind.

Deaf-blind
Can be accessible to those with some hearing.

People with learning difficulties
Can be accessible, although the technology involved may be off-putting.

Older people
Accessible to those who possess a tape player and are confident about dealing with the technology.

12, 28

RADIO

Radio is a popular medium. There are estimated to be 84.2 million radios in the UK – an average of nearly four per household.

Research by the Radio Advertising Bureau has shown that listeners see radio as an intimate, friendly medium. The majority of people under 45 years old listen to commercial stations, while BBC listeners are known to be especially loyal to individual stations.

There are several programmes specifically for disabled people and many local stations are anxious to serve disabled audiences more generally. It can be a relatively cheap medium through which to achieve wide coverage of a mixed audience or to target a more specific one.

One of radio's great advantages over other media is that it demands neither literacy nor good eyesight from its audiences. It can therefore reach a wide spectrum of people.

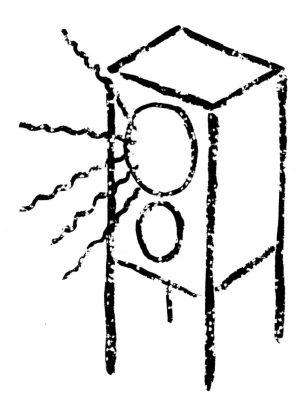

Accessibility of radio

People with literacy problems
Accessible. A major source of information.

Prelingually Deaf
Not accessible.

Hard of hearing
Not generally accessible.

Blind
Accessible. 62 per cent of people with visual impairment rate radio
as one of their most important sources of information.

Partially sighted
Accessible – see Blind.

Deaf-blind
Not generally accessible.

People with learning difficulties
Can be accessible, but likely to be less successful than
television / video.

Older people
Accessible, assuming no hearing impairment.

Chapter 12

13, 30, 41

MULTI-MEDIA

Information technology in a variety of forms can greatly assist people with sensory impairment or learning difficulties. This is because of the flexibility of the media involved and the fact that the information sources are not necessarily text-based and may involve images and sound.

Advances in computer technology and telecommunications are opening up almost limitless sources of information for anyone with the equipment and ability to access them. The numbers of computers and CD players in the UK are growing rapidly and people are becoming increasingly accustomed to accessing information through the technology available to them at home, at work, in education, and in places such as libraries.

Although PCs for people who are blind or partially sighted can be adapted to make information on the screen accessible, there is still a significant problem in using graphical user interfaces (GUIs) which tend to rely on icons and an awareness of the visual layout of the the screen. However some adaptive technology and software are already available, and it is hoped that current research will soon progress further towards solving the problems.

INFORMATION ON DISC

Providing information on disc allows individuals to access that information in the most convenient format for themselves, eg:

- as a print-out in an appropriate typeface and size;

- as text on screen at whatever size;

- as the spoken word through a speech synthesiser;

- as soft or paper braille.

However, since people with disabilities tend to have lower than average incomes it would be unwise to assume that they *all* have access to the hi-tech equipment needed to make use of discs or, indeed, any other multi-media-based information source.

THE INTERNET

The Internet is an international network of computers linked through the telephone system. It offers a vast source of information and a means of communication for people with the technology and knowledge to use it.

An increasing number of organisations maintain sites on the Internet. The majority of the information they provide is available for the cost of a local phone call.

Users can access and download a startling range of computer files, free software packages, video and audio files, provided they have the technological wherewithal. This basically involves a computer, a modem, a telephone line and the appropriate software.

Also, as the Internet becomes more accessible via cable technology the potential for combining it with television to create a flexible interactive source of information is increasing.

It is also possible to access the Internet through 'set-top boxes' which plug into a TV and provide a simple, cheap, albeit less flexible, alternative to access via a computer.

It is estimated that between 1 and 2 million people in the UK are connected to or use the Internet. As yet, little is known about who these people are or what they use the Internet for.

Extensive research and analysis of potential audiences is still needed before information providers are able to assess the Internet's true potential with any confidence.

Having said this, it is generally assumed that the majority of current Internet use is:

- for business purposes;

- by people under 35;

- by people in the higher socio-economic bracket.

E-mail

The full potential of the Internet is as yet relatively undiscovered. Electronic mail (e-mail) is by far the most commonly-used service.

Computer files of most types, including text in a variety of formats and digitised photographs, can be transmitted or downloaded when attached to e-mail files.

World Wide Web

The World Wide Web (WWW), a part of the Internet, was, until recently, mainly an editorial medium. It included text, pictures or photographs and a measure of typographical control which allowed Web sites to carry more attractive documents, and to provide 'click on' links with other pages or sites.

Recent developments promise a much more flexible WWW incorporating audio as well as visual material. To make use of these improved facilities, however, requires more powerful and more expensive equipment than that required simply to access the Internet.

Disadvantages of the Internet

- Access to the Internet relies on telephone lines and the speed of the modem. The more people who use the phone lines at any one time the more difficult it becomes to connect with a particular service. Or it may take longer to download information, which can result in higher telephone bills.

- Access to the Internet requires access to technology and knowledge that only a relatively small number of people currently possess. These people tend to fall into limited socio-economic and age ranges which may not be representative of a particular target audience.

- The Internet is a medium mainly used by 'information seekers', rather than those who might be described as 'information shy' or simply uncommitted. It is therefore not yet a proven means for supplying information effectively to a general audience.

Distribution of computerised information

Information can be sent to owners of computers by direct transmission down telephone lines, or on compact or floppy discs.

Those without access to their own computer can sometimes access information through organisations providing computerised information services to the public such as some libraries, Citizens Advice Bureaux, social service departments, disability information services etc.

However, to date little research has been done to establish exactly how common or effective these types of services are.

The availability of computerised sources of information should be announced in other media.

Accessibility of computer-based systems

People with literacy problems
Can be accessible, but only if the information given does not rely heavily on the written word.

Prelingually Deaf
Generally inaccessible if the information relies on the written word. As moving images and the software needed to access them become more common, providing information in BSL may eventually become a practical reality.

Hard of hearing
Accessible.

Blind
Accessible to people who have access to computers with voice synthesisers, voice cards, or facilities for renewable or soft braille read-outs.

Partially sighted
Accessible to those with computers with voice synthesisers, voice cards or large print facilities on screen or as a print-out.

Deaf-blind
Not generally accessible.

People with learning difficulties
Can be accessible, provided the information is presented in an accessible manner. People with learning difficulties often respond effectively to the interactive nature of computers.

Older people
Not accessible. Computer technology is less likely to be useful to the majority of older people because of lower incomes and/or a tendency to mistrust technology. This situation is changing, however, as generations grow up more accustomed to the use of computers in everyday life.

20, 42

COMPACT DISC TECHNOLOGY

The usefulness of CD (compact disc) technology for supplying information depends on the audience's access to the equipment needed to play the discs.

CD-ROM

CD-ROM (compact disc read-only memory), makes vast amounts of information readily available in a very compact format. It can also incorporate very high quality graphics, sound and moving images.

The medium is a great space-saver. Multi-volume encyclopedias or other bulky information sources can be condensed into disc format with the added convenience of very fast access to, and navigation around, the information.

CD-ROM is more expensive and less accessible than CD-I (compact disc interactive) because the user requires a computer to access it.

Other uses for CD-ROM include computer games and touch-screen kiosks. Touch-screen kiosks are an increasingly popular method of imparting information in public places such as shopping centres and hospitals. Their advantages are that the kiosks are unmanned and users are able to seek out the information they want when it suits them and at their own speed.

CD-Interactive

CD-I is easy to operate and also combines the speed of accessing information from a compact disc with the advantages of sound and very high quality moving images. Unlike CD-ROM, you do not need a computer to access CD-I. It simply requires a domestic television, a compact disc player and a simple control module/joystick.

Recent developments allow limited access to the Internet, and video on CD has better image quality than on video tape.

16

CD-I has particular potential for Deaf audiences because it can employ full-screen, full motion images, and is therefore an ideal medium for incorporating information in BSL. A trial project in Gateshead during the early 1990s demonstrated that the interactive nature of CD-I, coupled with information delivered in BSL, provided a very accessible medium for Deaf people.

The team responsible for the Gateshead project is currently developing the use of sign language on CD-I in three European languages, funded by the EC TIDE programme.

For a more general market, CD-I is an effective presentational tool, because of its high quality visual capability and interactive nature. It is increasingly used for training and for marketing purposes. And CD videos are likely to become increasingly popular in the future.

Disadvantages of CD-I

Although the equipment required to use CD-I is cheaper than that for CD-ROM, as with CD-ROM it is a relatively expensive medium for information providers.

It has not yet realised its full potential and is in competition with other multi-media technologies, especially in domestic situations. For these reasons the medium has not yet proved as popular with the mass market as originally expected.

Accessibility of CD

People with literacy problems
Accessible when it incorporates sound / voice-over.

Prelingually Deaf
Accessible if BSL is incorporated.

Hard of hearing
Accessible.

Blind
Can be accessible because CD-I can incorporate sound / voice-over. However, other media are likely to be more effective.

Partially sighted
Can be accessible – but see Blind.

Deaf-blind
Not accessible in general.

People with learning difficulties
Can be accessible because the mixed media facility and interactive nature of the technology allows 'readers' to access information by following their chosen path at their own speed.

Older people
Accessible in theory but in practice many older people may be reluctant to use the technology.

Chapter 13

13, 32, 47

TELEPHONES AND HELPLINES

Telephone response and helplines are useful sources of information or clarification for everyone, not just for those who have difficulty accessing standard information sources. They are especially useful to elderly or housebound people; those with visual impairment or literacy problems; or people who have physical disabilities which make it difficult to turn pages for instance.

The telephone can be used to offer immediate personalised help, advice or services on a one-to-one basis, or to deliver recorded information if this is appropriate.

Helplines can be relatively cheap to use, but because many people with disabilities have lower incomes than average, it will help them if you give a freephone number or if the service provider is able to ring them back.

> It is important to give effective publicity to help and enquiry lines.

Whether or not you are able to offer a textphone facility, all telephone operators should be briefed to expect calls from people with disabilities, and taught how to respond. Patience is an essential courtesy: some callers will need more time to give and receive information for instance, and some may be difficult to understand or have difficulty understanding the operator.

22

TEXTPHONES AND TYPETALK

To make telephone services accessible to Deaf or hard of hearing people and to people with speech impairments it is helpful to give a textphone number. Textphones enable people who are Deaf or hard of hearing to communicate using text via the telephone lines. The user types their message on a keyboard linked to the telephone and the message then appears on a small screen at the other end of the line.

Alternatively, its 17,500 registered users (as at April 1996) can use Typetalk, a service run by the RNID with funding from BT. For around the same price as it would cost to dial direct, people with textphones who are registered with the service can communicate with hearing people through the Typetalk operator. The operator translates between the spoken word and text. The service also allows hearing people who don't have access to a textphone to contact people who do.

To register with Typetalk, phone 0800 500 888.

The Typetalk number for textphone users already registered with the service is 0800 95 95 98. The number for hearing people using a normal phone is 0800 51 51 52. There is also an emergency textphone number for any textphone user – registered or not – this is 0800 112 999.

Note: Probably the best known make of textphone is the Minicom. For this reason 'Minicom' is often used as if it were synonymous with 'textphone' (much as 'Hoover' is often incorrectly used to mean 'vacuum cleaner').

VIDEOPHONES

23

Videophones are not commonly available as yet. Once they are, they will provide an invaluable communication aid for sign language users – giving deaf people the access to the telephone they have so long been denied.

Good picture quality is vitally important if sign language is to be transmitted effectively. Recent developments in improving image quality are making the use of videophones an increasingly viable possibility.

Pilot services have also shown videophones to be useful for people with learning difficulties. Being able to see the speaker and to have the opportunity to use visual clues can help reinforce the spoken message for people with limited understanding or limited verbal skills.

Accessibility of telephones

People with literacy problems
Accessible.

Prelingually Deaf
Only accessible via a textphone, and provided the user is confident reading and writing in English. Videophones will also improve accessibility in due course.

Hard of hearing
Accessible to some hearing aid users or those with less severe hearing impairment.

Blind
Accessible.

Partially sighted
Accessible.

Deaf-blind
Generally inaccessible.

People with learning difficulties
Limited accessibility. Some people with learning difficulties have problems using a telephone.

Older people
Accessible assuming the user has adequate hearing.

Chapter 14

SIGNAGE

Improving access for customers or visitors to your organisation –
be it an office, a shop, a railway station or a museum, leads to
happier customers and more of them.

The physical accessibility of buildings and services to wheelchair
users is an issue of general concern, but often little attention is
given to improving accessibility to people with sensory
impairment, literacy or learning difficulties.

Providing information about a person's surroundings is an
equally vital aspect of improving accessibility.

Signs, posters, notices and maps help people to navigate
independently through their environment. Clear signposting saves
everyone's time and is usually easy enough to achieve.

Messages can be given in a variety of formats:

- visual,

- tactile, and/or

- audible.

They should provide a clear and consistent sequence of
information. Where possible, it is helpful to provide information in
all formats at the same locations. A text sign which incorporates
tactile and braille information is more useful than three separate
signs in three different formats.

VISUAL SIGNS

Visual signs may include text, pictograms and/or symbols. You can
make them more accessible to people with visual impairment or
literacy or learning difficulties by ensuring they are easy to see,
easy to read and easy to understand.

Easy to see

At eye level wherever possible – between 1.4 and 1.6 metres above ground level is recommended. People in wheelchairs will benefit from signs between one and 1.5 metres above ground level. However, in some places signs may be more conspicuous above head height – e.g. in crowded areas such as large shops, airports or railway stations.

In consistent and logical places – signs should be where you would expect to find them; in the centre of a door at a height of 1.5 metres for instance; at points where decisions need to be made, such as junctions; or where information is needed to avoid confusion.

Well lit – whether by natural or artificial light.

Easily identified – too much 'visual noise' around or behind signs makes them difficult to spot. You should position signs where they don't have to compete with other visual information. The colour of the sign board should contrast with that of the background, whether the background is a brick wall, patterned wallpaper, green foliage, or whatever. Against dark backgrounds, use light coloured boards with dark text. Against light backgrounds use dark coloured boards with light text. Black on yellow or white, or vice versa, generally provide the best contrasts.

Indeed, visual contrast throughout the environment is beneficial to many people with visual impairment. In addition to prominent signage, the use of kerbstones, handrails, doorways, staircases and light switches in colours which contrast with their surroundings can help make many people's lives easier, and safer.

Easy to read

Use a clear typeface – so-called display faces are often difficult to read. The Royal National Institute for the Blind/Guide Dogs for the Blind (RNIB/GDBA) Joint Mobility Unit recommends sanserif typefaces such as Helvetica as particularly suitable for clear signage.

Choose an appropriate type size – this will depend on the distance from which the sign is to be read. If it is to be helpful to people with a visual impairment from 3 metres away, text should be between 100 and 170mm high. While from 1.5 metres, around 70 per cent of people with a visual impairment can read 50mm-high lettering so long as illumination, colour and contrast are good.

Use upper and lower case type – capitals are more difficult to read; upper and lower case provides much more distinctive, and therefore more legible, word shapes.

Use matt surfaces and materials – glare from reflective surfaces reduces legibility.

67 ℹ️ Note: Guidelines on designing for large print are also helpful when designing signs, posters and notices for display.

Easy to understand

Be concise – the fewer words the better.

Use plain language and keep the message clear and simple.

Be consistent – use colour, typeface and design style to link related signs or messages. And use readily recognisable symbols such as directional arrows, the international wheelchair symbol, P (for parking) and so on.

108

Allow enough time – when electronic means are used to provide information – for instance on a video monitor – it is important to allow enough time for the viewer or listener to absorb the information before it changes. This is especially important for people with literacy or learning difficulties.

TACTILE SIGNS

Tactile signs will help people with visual impairment. Tactile signs may use raised lettering or symbols which are readable by touch as well as by sight, or they may be in braille and then only accessible to braille readers. Or they can combine both systems.

Tactile signs could include labelling on doors, lift buttons or museum exhibits for instance, and include maps or diagrams presented in a raised format.

Tactile labelling at the top and bottom of staircases provides vital guidance for people with a visual impairment, but can also assist sighted people if there is poor visibility resulting from power failure or smoke for instance.

An added benefit of tactile signs is that they increase awareness of sighted people to the needs of people with visual impairment.

Tactile signs should be:

Embossed – rather than engraved. Lettering and symbols should be embossed by a minimum of 1mm above the surface of the sign.

Clear – lettering should be a minimum of 16mm high and should not exceed 50mm high.

Consistent – signs or messages should use readily recognisable symbols such as directional arrows, the international wheelchair symbol, P (for parking) and so on.

Easily located – in consistent, convenient positions where you would expect to find them; in the centre of doors at a height of 1.5 metres for instance, at points such as junctions where decisions need to made, or where information is needed to avoid confusion.

73

Braille signs

Braille signs should be in Grade 1 braille for single words, and in Grade 2 for longer notices.

As for visual and tactile signs, braille signs should be easy to locate and be in logical, convenient and consistent locations.

If the information is lengthy, such as an explanatory label in an exhibition, the panel should be mounted at 15 to 30 degrees from the horizontal.

Other tactile messages

Tactile surfaces are increasingly used to inform people with visual impairment about their surroundings. Blister pattern paving near dropped kerbs and pedestrian crossings, and corduroy-profile surfaces which warn of hazards such as approaching stairheads are common examples.

AUDIBLE SIGNS

Audible messages will help people with visual impairment, as well as the population in general. Obvious areas where audible announcements are particularly useful include:

- **Transport** – at stations, bus stops, airports etc.

- **Lifts** – announcing each floor, what's on that floor, and warnings about doors opening and closing for instance.

- **Entrances to buildings** – to inform visitors where they are, and what to do next (report to reception, take the lift to the required floor etc).

Audio tapes can also provide useful information for visitors to, for example, exhibitions, zoos or parks.

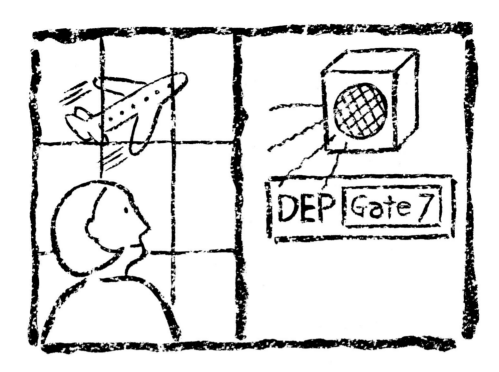

SIGNS OF THE FUTURE

Technology is currently being developed to provide people who have visual impairment with extra audible information about their environment. It may not be too long before infra-red transmitters in the street could give audible messages, via a receiver carried by a blind person, on the status of traffic lights, the location of a public phone box or the number of an approaching bus. And satellite navigation systems, based on those being developed for car drivers, will offer liberating possiblities for blind pedestrians through a receiver equipped with a speech output.

These systems are, however, still some way off becoming a practical reality.

Where now?

I hope the manual will have convinced you of the overwhelming need to adhere to the Informability principle of making information accessible to as wide an audience as possible.

In addition to the obvious moral arguments in favour of providing accessible information, in today's financially orientated world it also makes good business sense to target as large an audience as possible. Despite the inevitable problems, there are also rewards for individuals and organisations who make an effort to ensure their information is widely accessible. Well-informed people make well-informed decisions, are less of a burden on resources and are more likely to favour organisations which take their particular needs into account.

Now that the Disability Discrimination Act makes it unlawful for people who provide goods, facilities or services to discriminate against disabled people, information providers have a statutory duty to treat disabled people in the same way they would treat anyone else.

Treating people equally includes making sure that information is available to anyone who wants it in an accessible format:

- at the same time,
- to the same standards, and
- at the same price

as material offered to the rest of the population.

To avoid inadvertent discrimination it is essential that you get to know and understand your audiences' needs and preferences. Consultation with the end user is especially helpful if you want to be sure you make the right decisions.

You should make it a habit to:

- consult your audiences;
- prioritise which information needs particular attention;
- plan your strategy in advance;

- budget for a variety of formats;

- provide material in appropriate formats;

- publicise the available formats.

It is not acceptable to offer people with literacy problems or disabled people a lower standard of service. Indeed, any service provider who is deemed to have discriminated against a disabled person in how they offer a service can now be taken to court.

Looking ahead . . .

In the future, technology will be the biggest factor influencing how information is made available. The great advantage of electronic media is that it is the information receiver who controls their access to information by selecting the format most appropriate to their own needs. This will eventually take much of the onus off the information provider, who will simply need to make information available to everyone in an electronic format.

. . . and to the present

Nonetheless, for the time being very few people have access to such sophisticated technology, and even fewer have the ability to use it really effectively. This applies to the majority of information providers as well as to the information receivers. Electronic media do not yet offer all the solutions to all the problems of information dissemination. They can be useful adjuncts to existing channels of communication but are not, as yet, replacements.

It is still essential to use the more traditional, albeit less glamorous, media such as large print and braille, and to make sure you use them effectively.

And always remember that plain language continues to be the most important single influence on whether you communicate well or whether you communicate badly.

Statistics

Every effort has been made to ensure that the figures given are as up-to-date as possible.

However, since definitions of literacy and disability vary, as do methods of researching and calculating statistics, the figures are offered as general indicators of the size and needs of the various audiences rather than definitive totals.

All figures relate to the UK unless otherwise indicated.

GENERAL FIGURES

The population of the UK is:

58.4 million
(Office of National Statistics)

6.5 million
people in the UK are disabled i.e. over 10% of the population (ONS).

Under 2 per cent
of the adult population is registered as disabled (ONS).

2.4 million
people with disabilities are of working age (ONS).

31 per cent
of people with disabilities of working age are in employment (ONS).

People with disabilities are twice as likely to be unemployed as non–disabled people.
(Labour Force Survey 1993).

Under 5 per cent
of people with disabilities use wheelchairs (RADAR).

5 per cent
of cars bought each year are for use by disabled people.
(Consumers Association)

PEOPLE WITH LITERACY DIFFICULTIES

6.5 million
adults in England and Wales are estimated to have some degree of literacy difficulties; i.e. 16 per cent of the adult population (The Basic Skills Agency).

Figures are not available for Scotland and Northern Ireland, but the assumption is that the percentages would be similar (or possibly slightly lower) in these areas. This suggests that around

7.3 million

people in the UK as a whole are likely to have literacy difficulties.

The following figures are taken from The Basic Skills Agency's *Older and Younger: the basic skills of different age groups* (1995). However, the Agency warns that because this was a small scale survey "extrapolation to the population as a whole has to be treated with some caution".

Of those tested, the survey found that approximately

4 per cent

have very serious difficulties with reading, and a further

11 per cent

have poor or below average literacy skills.

PEOPLE WITH HEARING IMPAIRMENT

8.4 million

people have some form of hearing disability; i.e. over 14% of the population (RNID).

250,000

have a profound hearing loss (RNID).

62,000

use British Sign Language and make up the Deaf Community (BDA).

Only 45,500

are registered as deaf – of which 57% are aged 18–64 (Dept of Health, 1995).

Only 125,000

are registered as hard of hearing – of which 61% are aged over 75 (Dept of Health, 1995).

420,000

are unable to use a voice telephone (RNID).

4.2 million

have difficulty understanding speech on TV (BDA).

2 million

people (approximately) use a hearing aid (RNID).

17,500

are registered users of Typetalk (Typetalk).

54 per cent

of people over 60 are hard of hearing or deaf (RNID).

60 per cent

of people with hearing
impairment are over 70 (RNID).

45 per cent

of deaf people under 60 have
additional disabilities, mostly of a
physical nature (RNID).

77 per cent

of severely or profoundly deaf
people over 60 have additional
disabilities (RNID).

Deaf people are twice as likely to
be unemployed as the rest of the
population.

97 per cent

of deaf people have access to
colour television with teletext
(Deaf Broadcasting Council).

PEOPLE WITH VISUAL IMPAIRMENT

Except where indicated, figures
in this section come from the
RNIB's survey *Blind and
Partially sighted adults in
Britain* (HMSO 1991) and only
relate to people over 16 years old.

1.1 million

people are eligible to be
registered as blind or partially
sighted, of which 315,782 are
registered (RNIB 1996).

1.7 million

are unable to read standard print
with any ease.

Only 23 per cent

of people living in private
households who are registrable
are in fact registered.

Only 4 per cent

of blind people have no light
perception at all.

90 per cent

of people with a visual
impairment are over 60.

500,000

people with a visual impairment
are over 75.

72 per cent

of people with visual impairment
are women. This is because visual
impairment is more common
among older people and women
live longer on average than men.

Only 56 per cent

of people with visual impairment
are married (compared to 74% of
the general population).

117

36 per cent

of blind people *can* read large print but only

12 per cent

do so regularly.

75 per cent

of partially sighted people *can* read large print but

only 29 per cent

do so regularly.

19,000

can read braille (approximately 2% of the registrable visually impaired population).

13,000

blind people are *active* braille readers.

22 per cent

of blind people of working age use braille.

Nearly 50 per cent

of blind people in employment use braille.

1,000

people read Moon.

346,000

people with visual impairment live alone.

90 per cent

of blind and partially sighted people 'watch' television.

60 per cent

rate television as a major source of information.

62 per cent

rate radio as a major source of information.

24 per cent

of people who are blind use information on audio tape.

6 per cent

of people who are partially sighted use information on audio tape.

25 per cent

of blind and partially sighted people don't have a telephone.

10,000 to 20,000

blind and partially sighted people could access the Internet according to a recent RNIB estimate.

PEOPLE WHO ARE DEAF–BLIND

250,000

people in the UK have both visual and hearing impairment (RNIB).

23,000

are severly affected by both impairments (Sense).

22 per cent

of people under 60 with a visual impairment also have hearing impairment.

And an estimated

45 per cent

of people over 75 with a visual impairment also have hearing impairment (RNIB).

PEOPLE WITH LEARNING DIFFICULTIES

1 million

people in the UK have learning difficulties (Mencap).

350 words

constitute the Makaton core vocabulary.

7000 words

constitute the Makaton resource vocabulary.

Mental illness

6 million

people per year in England are diagnosed as having a mental health problem (MIND).

245,000

are admitted to hospital due to mental illness every year in England (MIND).

OLDER PEOPLE

9 million

people are over 65 years old; i.e. over 15 per cent of the population (ONS).

6 million

people are over 70; i.e. over 10 per cent of the population (ONS).

2.3 million

people are over 80; i.e. almost 4 per cent of the population. 70 per cent of them are women (ONS).

50 per cent

of people with disabilities are over 70 (RADAR).

Over 33 per cent

of households are headed by someone over 60 years old (General Household Survey 1993, HMSO).

17 per cent

of households consist of one person over 60 living alone (General Household Survey 1993, HMSO).

95 per cent

of people over 65 years old live in private housing. Of these:

38 per cent

live alone;

46 per cent

live just with a partner; and

8 per cent

live with relatives (General Household Survey 1993, HMSO).

97 per cent

of people over 65 wear glasses (RNIB).

33 per cent

of people over 65 have hearing difficulties (RNID).

100 million

people in Europe are over 65 at present (Office for Official Publications of the European Communities, 1994).

25 per cent

of Europeans will be over 60 by the year 2020. (Office for Official Publications of the European Communities, 1994).

90 per cent

of older people have their own telephone.

97.6 per cent

have access to a telephone.

Addresses

Access to Information and Reading Services (AIRS)
Gateshead Libraries and Arts
Gateshead Central Library
Prince Consort Road
Gateshead NE8 4LN
Tel: 0191 477 3478
Fax: 0191 477 7852
Textphone: 0191 478 2060 (Minicom)

Action for Blind People
14-16 Verney Road
London SE16 3DZ
Tel: 0171 732 8771
Fax: 0171 639 0948

**ADAIP
(Alliance of Disability Advice and Information Providers)**
c/o DIAL UK
Park Lodge
St Catherine's Hospital
Tickhill Road
Doncaster DN4 8QN
Tel: 01302 310123
Fax: 01302 310404
Textphone: 01302 310123

Age Concern England
Astral House
1268 London Road
London SW16 4ER
Tel: 0181 679 8000
Fax: 0181 679 6069
Textphone: 0181 679 2832 (Minicom)

Age Concern Cymru
4th Floor
1 Cathedral Road
Cardiff CF1 9SD
Tel: 01222 371566
Fax: 01222 399562
E-mail: accymru@ace.org.uk

Age Concern Scotland
113 Rose Street
Edinburgh EH2 3DT
Tel: 0131 220 3345
Fax: 0131 220 2779
Textphone: 0181 679 2832

Basic Skills Agency, The
Commonwealth House
1-19 New Oxford Street
London WC1A 1NU
Tel: 0171 405 4017
Fax: 0171 404 5038

BBC Focus
The Learning Zone
Room EG 12
Woodlands
80 Wood Lane
London W12 0TT
Tel: 0181 576 2755
Fax: 0181 749 1647

British Council of Organisations of Disabled People (BCODP)
Litchurch Plaza
Litchurch Lane
Derby DE24 8AA
Tel: 01332 295551
Fax: 01332 295580
Textphone: 01332 295581

121

British Deaf Association (BDA)
1-3 Worship Street
London EC2A 2AB
Tel: 0171 588 3520
Fax: 0171 588 3527
Textphone: 0171 588 3529

British Dyslexia Association
98 London Road
Reading
Berkshire RG1 5AU
Tel: 01189 662677
Fax: 01189 351927
Helpline: 01189 668271

British Institute of Learning Disabilities (BILD)
Wolverhampton Road
Kidderminster
Worcestershire DY10 3PP
Tel: 01562 850251
Fax: 01562 851970

BT Age and Disability Unit
Room 103
Procter House
100-110 High Holborn
London WC1V 6LD
Tel: 0345 581456 (local rate)
Fax: 0171 728 8589
Textphone: 0800 243 123 (CCITT)

Central Office of Information
Hercules Road
London SE1 7DU
Tel: 0171 928 2345
Fax: 0171 928 5037

Confederation of Tape Information Services (COTIS)
c/o RNIB Transcription Centre
Northwest
67 High Street
Tarporley
Cheshire CW6 0DP
Tel: 01829 733351
Fax: 01829 732408

Council for the Advancement of Communication with Deaf People (CACDP)
Pelaw House
School of Education
University of Durham
Durham DH1 1TA
Tel: 0191 374 3607
Fax: 0191 374 3605
Text answerphone:
0191 374 7864 (Minicom)

Deaf Broadcasting Council
70 Blacketts Wood Drive
Chorleywood
Rickmansworth
Hertfordshire WD3 5QQ
Fax: 01923 283127
Textphone: 01923 283 127

DIAL UK
Park Lodge
St Catherine's Hospital
Tickhill Road
Doncaster DN4 8QN
Tel: 01302 310123
Fax: 01302 310404
Textphone: 01302 310123

DIEL
(Advisory Committee on
Telecommunications for
Disabled and Elderly People)
Room 1/1
50 Ludgate Hill
London EC4M 7JJ
Tel: 0171 634 8770
Fax: 0171 634 8845
Textphone: 0171 634 8769
(Minicom)

Disability Action
2 Annadale Avenue
Belfast BT7 3JH
Tel: 01232 491011
Fax: 01232 491627
Textphone: 01232 645779

Disability Matters Ltd
Berkeley House
West Tytherley
Wiltshire SP5 1NF
Tel: 01794 341144
Fax: 01794 341777

Disability Resource Team
Bedford House
125-133 Camden High Street
London NW1 7JR
Tel: 0171 482 5062
Fax: 0171 482 0796
Textphone: 0171 482 5062/5299

Disability Scotland
Princes House
5 Shandwick Place
Edinburgh EH2 4RG
Tel: 0131 229 8632
Fax: 0131 229 5168
Textphone: 0131 229 8632

Disability Wales/Anabledd Cymru
Llys Ifor
Crescent Road
Caerphilly CF83 1XL
Tel: 01222 887325
Fax: 01222 888702
Textphone: 01222 887325 (Minicom)
E-mail: dwac@mcr1.poptel.org.uk

Disabled Living Foundation
380-384 Harrow Road
London W9 2HU
Tel: 0171 289 6111
Fax: 0171 266 2922
E-mail: dlf@atlas.co.uk

Employers Forum on Disability
Nutmeg House
60 Gainsford Street
London SE1 2NY
Tel: 0171 403 3020
Fax: 0171 403 0404

GLAD
(Greater London Association
of Disabled People)
336 Brixton Road
London SW9 7AA
Tel: 0171 274 0107
Fax: 0171 274 7840
Textphone: 0171 274 0107

Hearing Concern
7-11 Armstrong Road
London W3 7JL
Tel: 0181 743 1110
Fax: 0181 742 9043
Textphone: 0181 742 9151

Help the Aged
St James's Walk
Clerkenwell Green
London EC1R 0BE
Tel: 0171 253 0253
Fax: 0171 250 4474

London Deaf Access Project (LDAP)
1-3 Worship Street
London EC2A 2AB
Tel: 0171 588 3522
Fax: 0171 588 3526
Textphone: 0171 588 3528

Makaton Vocabulary Development Project
31 Firwood Drive
Camberley
Surrey GU15 3QD
Tel: 01276 61390
Fax: 01276 681368

MENCAP
MENCAP National Centre
123 Golden Lane
London EC1Y 0RT
Tel: 0171 454 0454
Fax: 0171 608 3254

MIND
Granta House
15-19 Broadway
London E15 4BQ
Tel: 0181 519 2122
Fax: 0181 519 1725
Information line:
0181 522 1728 (London);
0345 660163 (outside London)

NACAB (National Association of Citizens' Advice Bureaux)
115 Pentonville Road
London N1 9LZ
Tel: 0171 833 2181
Fax: 0171 833 4371

NAIDEX
Reed Exhibition Companies (UK)
Oriel House
26 The Quadrant
Richmond
Surrey TW9 1DL
Tel: 0181 910 7873
Fax: 0181 910 7926

National Council of Voluntary Organisations
Regent's Wharf
81 All Saints Street
London N1 9RL
Tel: 0171 713 6161
Fax: 0171 713 6300
Textphone: 0171 278 1289
(Minicom)

National Deafblind League

18 Rainbow Court
Paston Ridings
Peterborough PE4 6UP
Tel: 01733 573511
(voice and Minicom)
Fax: 01733 325353
Textphone: 01733 321982 (Qwerty)

**National Deafblind League
Scottish Office**

21 Alexandra Avenue
Lenzie
Glasgow G66 5BG
Tel: 0141 777 6111
Fax: 0141 775 3311

**National Deaf Children's Society
(NDCS)**

15 Dufferin Street
London EC1Y 8PD
Tel: 0171 250 0123
Fax: 0171 251 5020
Textphone: 0171 250 0123

**National Federation
of the Blind**

Unity House
Smyth Street
Westgate
Wakefield
West Yorkshire WF1 1ER
Tel: 01924 291313
Fax: 01924 200244

National Information Forum

Post Point 228
BT Procter House
100-110 High Holborn
London WC1V 6LD
Tel: 0171 404 3846
Fax: 0171 404 3849

**National Library for
the Blind**

Cromwell Road
Bredbury
Stockport SK6 2SG
Tel: 0161 494 0217
Fax: 0161 406 6728

Partially Sighted Society

PO Box 322
Doncaster DN1 2XA
Tel: 01302 323132
Fax: 01302 368998

People First

207-215 Kings Cross Road
London WC1X 9DB
Tel: 0171 713 6400
Fax: 0171 833 1880

Pia

37 Charles Street
Cardiff CF1 4EB
Tel: 01222 222782
Fax: 01222 222383
E-mail: braille@pia.co.uk

Plain English Campaign

PO Box 3
New Mills
Stockport SK12 4QP
Tel: 01663 744409
Fax: 01663 747038

Plain Language Commission

29 Stoneheads
Whaley Bridge
Stockport SK12 7BB
Tel: 01663 733177
Fax: 01663 735135

Royal Association for Disability and Rehabilitation (RADAR)

12 City Forum
250 City Road
London EC1V 8AF
Tel: 0171 250 3222
Fax: 0171 250 0212
Textphone: 0171 250 4119 (Minicom)

Royal Association in aid of Deaf People (RAD)

27 Old Oak Road
Acton
London W3 7HN
Tel: 0181 743 6187
Fax: 0181 740 6551
Textphone: 0181 749 7561

Royal National Institute for Deaf People (RNID)

19-23 Featherstone Street
London EC1Y 8SL
Tel: 0171 296 8000
Fax: 0171 296 8199
Textphone: 0171 296 8001 (Minicom)

RNID Scotland

9 Clairmont Gardens
Glasgow G3 7LW
Tel: 0141 332 0343
Fax: 0141 331 2640
Textphone: 0141 332 5023

RNID Northern Ireland

Information Department
Wilton House
5 College Square North
Belfast BT1 6AR
Tel: 01232 329738
(voice/answerphone)
Fax: 01232 312032
Textphone: 01232 331716
(text/answerphone)

Royal National Institute for the Blind (RNIB)

224 Great Portland Street
London W1N 6AA
Tel: 0171 388 1266
Fax: 0171 388 2034

RNIB Customer Services

PO Box 173
Peterborough PE2 6WS
Tel: 0345 023153
(calls charged at local rate)
Fax: 01733 371555

RNIB/GDBA Joint Mobility Unit

224 Great Portland Street
London W1N 6AA
Tel: 0171 387 2233
Fax: 0171 388 3160

RNIB Production & Distribution Centre

PO Box 173
Peterborough PE2 6WS
Tel: 01733 370777
Fax: 01733 371555

RNIB Resources Centre

9 Viewfield Place
Stirling FK8 1NL
Tel: 01786 451 752
Fax: 01786 462 336

RNIB Scottish Branch

10 Magdala Crescent
Edinburgh EH12 5BE
Tel: 0131 313 1498
Fax: 0131 313 1875

Scope (formally The Spastics Society)

12 Park Crescent
London W1N 4EQ
Tel: 0171 636 5020
Fax: 0171 436 2601
Helpline: 0800 626216

Scottish Association for the Deaf

Moray House College
Holyrood Road
Edinburgh EH8 8AQ
Tel: 0131 557 0591
Fax: 0131 557 6922
Textphone: 0131 558 3390

Scottish Association of Sign Language Interpreters

31 York Place
Edinburgh EH1 3HP
Tel: 0131 557 6370
Fax: 0131 557 4110
Textphone: 0131 557 6370

Scottish Braille Press

Craigmillar Park
Edinburgh EH16 5NB
Tel: 0131 662 4445
Fax: 0131 662 1968

Sense

11-13 Clifton Terrace
London N4 3SR
Tel: 0171 272 7774
Fax: 0171 272 6012
Textphone: 0171 272 9648

Share the Vision

36 Circular Road
Castlerock
County Londonderry BT51 4XA
Tel: 01265 848303
Fax: 01265 848003
E-mail: p.craddock@bbcnc.org.uk

Talking Newspaper Enterprises Ltd (TNEL)

National Recording Centre
Heathfield
East Sussex TN21 8DB
Tel: 01435 866102
Fax: 01435 865422
E-mail:
101761.167@compuserve.com

Typetalk

John Wood House
Glacier Building
Harrington Road
Brunswick Business Park
Liverpool L3 4DF
Tel: 0151 709 9494
Fax: 0151 709 8119
Textphone: 0800 500 888
(registration helpline)

**UKABP (UK Association
of Braille Producers)**

108 High Street
Hurstpierpoint
West Sussex BN6 9PX
Tel: 01273 834321
Fax: 01273 833744

Wales Council for the Blind

3rd Floor
Shand House
20 Newport Road
Cardiff CF2 1DB
Tel: 01222 473954
Fax: 01222 455710

**Wales Council for the
Deaf/Cyngor Cymru i'r Byddar**

Maritime Offices
Woodland Terrace
Maesycoed
Pontypridd
Mid Glamorgan CF37 1DZ
Tel: 01443 485687
Fax: 01443 408555
Textphone: 01443 485686
(minicom)

Glossary of terms

The Glossary includes words, phrases and abbreviations used in the manual plus others in common use which relate to disability.

Some expressions are disliked by or offensive to certain groups or individuals, so guidance on terms to be avoided is also offered.

It is not possible to list all variations of preference, but as a general rule labels such as the disabled, the blind, a spastic should be avoided as they use disability to define a group or individual and encourage stereotyping. It is preferable to say people with disabilities or disabled people, people who are blind, a person with cerebral palsy.

Nor should you use words which suggest reliance upon others or invite pity. 'Handicapped', for instance, is offensive to some disabled people with its connotations of cap-in-hand. You should also avoid expressions such as 'victim of', 'suffers from', 'afflicted by', or 'confined to a wheelchair'.

Obviously, you should not use expressions such as 'blind as a bat', 'deaf and dumb', or words which have assumed a derogatory meaning such as 'spastic', 'cripple' or 'retarded'.

The following words and phrases are defined as we've used them in this manual.

access
the ability to retrieve or receive information.

accessible medium
any medium which assists access to information.

Audetel
a TIDE-sponsored project to develop audio description on television in Europe.

audio description
spoken description of images on the TV screen to assist comprehension by people with visual impairment.

Basic Skills Agency, The
a national development agency for literacy, numeracy and related basic skills in England and Wales (formerly the Adult Literacy Basic Skills Unit).

BBC Focus
a special television service broadcast as part of BBC's The Learning Zone during the 'quiet hours' of 4a.m.–6a.m. It offers non-profit-making organisations the opportunity to make and broadcast specialist programmes to specific audiences.

BDA
British Deaf Association.

blind
with little or no useful sight.

Blissymbolics
a symbol system which allows a small number of basic shapes to be used to create a vocabulary of almost infinite size.

braille
a tactile alphabet used regularly by 13,000 people who are blind.

British Sign Language (BSL)
the indigenous visual gestural language used by the Deaf community in the UK. BSL is the fourth indigenous language in the UK after English, Welsh and Gaelic.

BSL
British Sign Language.

CD
compact disc.

CD-I
compact disc interactive.

CD-ROM
compact disc read-only memory.

Ceefax
BBC teletext service.

closed subtitles
subtitling which gives the viewer the option of whether to display the subtitles or not.

COI – Central Office of Information
an executive agency dedicated to enhancing the effectiveness of government's communication with its many audiences.

culturally Deaf
people who consider themselves part of a linguistic, cultural minority group: i.e. the Deaf community.

DDA
Disability Discrimination Act 1995.

Deaf/deaf
the accepted convention among the BDA and academic institutions in the field use Deaf (capital D) to refer to people who have a positive deaf identity and are culturally Deaf (these would normally be people who are prelingually deaf); deaf (lower case d) refers to people who see their deafness as a medical (rather than cultural) condition and is sometimes also used when referring to people who are hard of hearing (e.g. 'He's slightly deaf').

deaf and dumb
offensive to deaf people. Use deaf without speech.

Deaf community
those who are culturally Deaf; generally those who are prelingually Deaf, use BSL as their first language, and share a sense of community, i.e. around 62,000 people. Some hearing people with Deaf families also consider themselves part of this community.

deafened
having become deaf (as opposed to born deaf) due to ageing, illness or trauma.

Deaf without speech
people who have no useful hearing and whose normal method of communication is by signs, finger-spelling or writing.

Deaf with speech
people who, even with a hearing aid, have little or no useful hearing but whose normal method of communication is by speech and lipreading.

disability

the Disability Discrimination Act defines disability as: a physical or mental impairment which has a substantial and long-term adverse effect on a person's ability to carry out normal day-to-day activities.

The British Council of Organisations of Deaf People (BCODP) defines it as: the loss or limitation of opportunities to take part in the normal life of the community on an equal level with others due to physical and social barriers.

The International Classification of Impairments, Disabilities and Handicaps (ICIDH, part of the World Health Organisation) defines it as: any restriction or lack (resulting from an impairment) of ability to perform an activity in the manner or within the range considered normal for a human being.

The distinction between the BCODP and ICIDH definitions is important in that the first relates disability to society's failure to give disabled people truly equal rights; whereas the second, rejected by many disabled people, focuses on the individual and their perceived inadequacy.

disabled person

someone with a disability (see above). Some people object to the term disabled people and prefer people with disabilities; there is no consensus as to an acceptable alternative.

disabled toilet

a lavatory which is out of commission or not functioning; always use 'accessible toilet'.

finger spelling

a method of communication for people with hearing impairment involving spelling out words using the hands.

GUI

Graphical User Interface.

handicap

a word to be avoided if possible. Most disabled people object to the term as it conjures up images of competition, or begging. Handicap is defined by the ICIDH as: a disadvantage for a given individual, resulting from an impairment or disability, that limits or prevents the fulfilment of a role (depending on age, sex and social and cultural factors) for that individual.

hard of hearing
having some useful hearing with or without a hearing aid, and whose normal method of communication is by speech-listening and lipreading.

hearing dog
a dog trained to alert deaf people to everyday sounds such as the telephone, doorbell, cooker timer or smoke alarm.

illiterate
unable to read at all.

impairment
defined by the ICIDH as: any loss or abnormality of psychological, physiological or anatomical structure or function. This also includes sensory impairment.

induction loop
generally a loop of wire round a room or area which amplifies sound for wearers of hearing aids, provided their aid is switched to its 'T' setting. A small version can also be worn round the neck.

Informability
the principle of ensuring information is made accessible to as wide an audience as possible.

Informability Unit
the part of the COI responsible for helping the public sector make its information more accessible.

infra-red system
has a similar effect to an induction loop, but is more sophisticated and requires the wearing of a special receiver. Often used in cinemas and theatres.

invalid
avoid; it can be construed as meaning 'not valid'.

ITC
Independent Television Commission.

large print

used in this guide to mean type which is 14pt or larger. Large print books commonly use 14pt type and RNIB recommends this as the minimum print size for material intended for blind and partially sighted readers.

learning difficulty

a condition in which a person's brain does not develop as fast or as fully as that of a person with no learning difficulty. Degree of learning difficulty may vary but it is a permanent condition. The term should be used in preference to mental handicap.

learning disability

Mencap-preferred term for people with learning difficulties.

Learning Zone, The

BBC television service broadcast in the quiet hours from 2a.m. to 6a.m.

lip reader

someone who uses lip reading to help them communicate.

lip speaker

someone who uses clear lip movements in order to interpret the spoken word for the benefit of lip readers.

Makaton

a symbol system used to assist people with learning difficulties or those who have acquired communication and literacy impairments.

mentally handicapped

avoid; people with learning difficulties is the preferred term.

mental illness

condition in which a person has psychiatric and/or emotional problems. Mental illness can be treated and is temporary in the majority of cases.

Minicom

a text telephone which allows people who are deaf to use the phone lines.

Moon

a simple tactile alphabet based on the Roman alphabet, simpler to read than braille, especially for those with less sensitive fingers. Not in widespread use.

ONS

Office of National Statistics (originally the Office of Population Censuses and Surveys).

open subtitles
subtitles which appear on the screen automatically, so viewers have no option but to see them.

palantype
a system of inputting words into a special machine which then relays the text onto a screen for the benefit of deaf or hard of hearing people.

palantypist
someone who operates a palantype machine.

prelingually deaf
born deaf or having become deaf before learning to speak.

profoundly deaf
with no useful hearing. The term is also usually used refer to people who are deaf and without speech (as opposed to the offensive and out-dated "deaf and dumb").

Rebus
a symbol system using mainly stylised pictures and often used in conjunction with Makaton.

RNIB
Royal National Institute for the Blind.

RNID
Royal National Institute for Deaf People.

sign language
the generic term for the language of signs and gesture.

Sign Supported English (SSE)
a signing system which incorporates elements of BSL, fingerspelling and the grammatical structure of spoken English.

soft braille
a renewable brailling system based on a series of small movable rods which allows braille to be created, read and erased using a computer.

standard print
used here to refer to type which is 12pt or smaller – usually between 8 and 10pt for general readership.

teletext
generic name for textual information on television. Page 888 carries subtitles.

Teletext
ITV's teletext service.

TIDE
Telematics applications for the integration of Disabled and Elderly people: a project funded by the European Union to encourage development of technology.

tone indexing
the addition of tone codes to audio tapes which assist in identifying particular sections of the recording for people with tone index units attached to their tape machines.

Total Communication (TC)
a flexible approach to communication for deaf people incorporating sign language, residual hearing, fingerspelling, reading, speech and gestures.

Typetalk
RNID-run, BT-funded service whereby deaf and hard of hearing people can communicate by textphone with hearing people using standard telephones. The service has 17,500 registered users (as at April 1996).

Usher syndrome
an hereditary condition which causes some people born deaf or partially hearing to lose their sight in adolescence. Often a progressive condition.

Viewdata
a screen-based information system.

visually impaired
blind or partially sighted.

voice card
a computer card which allows the computer to deliver information through speech.

voice synthesiser
a computer add-on which converts text into speech.

WWW
World Wide Web

Index

For reasons of economy, the index appears in a smaller type size than text throughout the rest of the manual.
For people who do not find the smaller point size legible, we have provided a detailed contents list at the beginning and an easy-to-follow cross referencing system throughout the manual.

Printed in the UK for HMSO
Dd. 302168 11/96 C30 20249